spontaneous nature
— on the bus

AN OPEN LIFE

Why I feel like

having a steady life so much?
Oct. 2. 手

Oct. 1 , 1991年

书 Duthie

Eaton , Food Fair

WORKS OF JOSEPH CAMPBELL

WRITINGS

A Skeleton Key to Finnegans Wake (with Henry Morton Robinson)

The Hero with a Thousand Faces

The Masks of God: Primitive Mythology

The Masks of God: Oriental Mythology

The Masks of God: Occidental Mythology

The Masks of God: Creative Mythology

The Flight of the Wild Gander: Explorations in the Mythological Dimension

Myths to Live By

The Mythic Image

Historical Atlas of World Mythology
  I. The Way of the Animal Powers
  II. The Way of the Seeded Earth

The Inner Reaches of Outer Space: Metaphors, Myth & Religion

EDITED

The Portable Arabian Nights

Spirit and Nature: Papers From the Eranos Yearbooks (6 volumes)

Myths, Dreams, and Religion

The Portable Jung

EDITED AND COMPLETED (*from posthuma of Heinrich Zimmer*)

Myths and Symbols in Indian Art and Civilization

The King and the Corpse: Tales of the Soul's Quest of Evil

Philosophies of India

The Art of Indian Asia (2 volumes)

AN OPEN LIFE

Joseph Campbell

IN CONVERSATION WITH

Michael Toms

FOREWORD BY

Jean Erdman Campbell

SELECTED AND EDITED BY

John M. Maher and Dennie Briggs

PERENNIAL LIBRARY

Harper & Row, Publishers, New York
Grand Rapids, Philadelphia, St. Louis, San Francisco
London, Singapore, Sydney, Tokyo, Toronto

First PERENNIAL LIBRARY edition published 1990

Library of Congress Cataloging-in-Publication Data

Campbell, Joseph, 1904–1987
    An open life / Joseph Campbell in conversation with
Michael Toms : foreword by Jean Erdman Campbell :
selected and edited by John M. Maher and Dennie
Briggs. — 1st Perennial Library ed.
        p.   cm.
    Reprint. Originally published: Burdett, N.Y. : Larson
Publications. c1988.
    Includes index.
    ISBN 0-06-097295-5
    1. Campbell, Joseph, 1904–1987—Interviews.
2. Religion 3. Myth. I. Toms, Michael. II. Maher,
John M.   III. Briggs, Dennie.   IV. Title.
    BL48.C325   1990
    291—dc20   89-33033

---

90 91 92 93 94 FG 10 9 8 7 6 5 4 3 2 1

Photo page 20 courtesy of Sarah Lawrence College.
Additional photos by Jim Lerager, reprinted courtesy of
New Dimensions Foundation.

*T*O HONOR the memory and preserve
the legacy of Joseph Campbell,
friend and mentor.

CONTENTS

Editors' note   9
Foreword: Jean Erdman Campbell   11
Introduction: Michael Toms   13

One: Myth as Metaphor   21
Two: The God Denied   55
Three: The Social Contract   99
Four: An Open Life   119

Index   131
About New Dimensions   139

EDITORS' NOTE

THIS BOOK is a compilation of interviews which took place over a ten-year period, beginning in 1975. We intended to present the finished work to Joseph Campbell on his eighty-fourth birthday, which was to have been celebrated at an annual workshop with Chungliang Al Huang, at the Esalen Institute. Joseph's untimely death in October, 1987, however, cut short our plans; yet, it also determined the importance of publishing these conversations. Along with his writings, they stand as a celebration of the human spirit and a life well lived.

We would like to thank Michael Toms, who hosted these programs and who entrusted the work to us. Also, our deep appreciation goes to Jean Erdman Campbell, who generously encouraged our endeavors. Finally, we would like to thank Bob Briggs for his editorial comments and suggestions.

JOHN MAHER
DENNIE BRIGGS
SAN FRANCISCO, CALIFORNIA

*T*HROUGHOUT his long career, Joseph Campbell endeavored to communicate his understanding of myth—his passion. And he tirelessly pursued the task he had set himself. Besides his books and lectures, there were workshops and interviews, which he eagerly welcomed because he believed scholarship should not mean isolation; he delighted in talking to people who shared his interests. In particular, he looked forward to his meetings with Michael Toms whose interviews had the warmth of genial conversation. Their first meeting took place in 1975, and over the next twelve years, Joseph and Michael met regularly to discuss the advances in mythological scholarship.

I am pleased that these meetings are now available in book form. Along with his other works, they are Joseph's legacy to us, and a record of the friendship he shared with Michael Toms.

JEAN ERDMAN CAMPBELL
HONOLULU, HAWAII

"AWESOME" is the word most appropriate to the feeling I remember after encountering Joseph Campbell's *The Hero with a Thousand Faces*. For one person to have assembled such a wealth of mythic knowledge from so many diverse cultures, and in one book, was simply astonishing. Later, I came to learn that Joseph had spent four years of his life writing that book, which has since become a classic in mythology and is now enjoying a rebirth with the resurgence of interest in Joseph's work. *Hero* was for me a life-enhancing experience, because it validated my own intuitive leanings and confirmed the path I had already chosen for my life.

I first actually met Joseph at a seminar in San Francisco in 1974 where he was eloquently describing the symbology of the Tarot Deck. My excitement was palpable in anticipation.

Tall, spirited, and noble like the hero he so often wrote about, Joseph presented an air of graceful and gentlemanly elegance. He knew where he had been and where he was going, as befitted someone who "follows his bliss," living his vision actively in the world. Notwithstanding his conservative, dark blue suit and stately carriage, Joseph clearly fit the role of planetary elder—like a primitive shaman telling mythic tales around the fire—as he proceeded to share openly his well-

earned wisdom with an overeager yet well-meaning interviewer. Soon, Joseph's natural charity won out and we were
simply soaring, as one unit, personalities dissolved in the
limitless sky of ideas. He possessed the rare gift of distilling
wisdom from a bottomless well of information and knowledge, and I was entranced—thoroughly captivated by the
master. And so it was with our first encounter. He later came to
call our meetings "religious exercise."

Thus began our vision quest together in dialogue, exploring
humanity's past, probing the dark depths and ascending the
glorious heights. This was not a musty, murky, and stilted
learning expedition so common to the halls of academia, but
rather an exciting and visionary leap into the future with a
master guide using the maps of the past to light the way. My
experience with traditional education was dismal, though I
can recall a few dedicated teachers who were compelling
enough to get my attention. With Joseph, I was carried into a
realm far beyond any of my previous learning experiences. His
words were like water to a thirsty mind.

Joseph's own life was rich with examples of the mythic lore
he so dearly loved to recount, especially in its seemingly small
synchronicities. There were, for example, his fortuitous meeting with J. Krishnamurti in 1924 on a passenger liner to
Europe; his chance encounter with Adelle Davis on a boat to
Cuba (long before she became famous as a nutritionist), who
later helped him out of a deep depression in San Francisco
during the 1930s; and the special times he spent with John
Steinbeck in Pacific Grove in 1932, which he described in a
1977 article in *Esquire* magazine:

"A beautiful time; we were all in heaven. The world had
dropped out. We weren't the dropouts; the world was the
dropout. We were in a halcyon situation, no movement,
just floating. Just great. . . . So I'm coasting along, trying
to find where I am, crazy on Spengler. Ed Ricketts [made
famous by Steinbeck's *Cannery Row*] was an intertidal
biologist. We'd go out and collect hundreds of starfish,

sea cucumbers, things like that, between high and low tides, furnishing animals for biology classes and schools."

There was also his wondrously free Alaskan jaunt that same year, a description of which also appeared in the same article.

"Ed made an arrangement to go to Alaska on a small boat. Great! What else is there to do? So we cruised up the Inside Passage from Seattle to Juneau . . . well, the Inside Passage was gorgeous. We sat on the stern as that little launch went out into the waters of Puget Sound, off for six weeks, much of which we'd spend at an absolutely uninhabited island gathering animals while Ed made notes. The cost: twenty-five cents a day for the whole crew. We would pull into the port, all the canneries were closed, the fishing fleets immobilized—they'd *throw* salmon at us. Put your hand in the water and pull fish out. Just an idyll. And the towns were supposed to be dead and they were the most *living* things. There's nothing like living when you're not living with a direction but just enjoying the glory of the moment. That's what we were doing."

His decision at age thirty to retire to Woodstock and read the classics for four years was another example of his free-wheeling spirit and commitment to pursuing his vision. As he wrote in *The Hero*, "Whether small or great, and no matter what the stage or grade of life, the Call rings up the curtain, always, on a mystery of transfiguration—a rite, or moment, of spiritual passage, which, when complete, amounts to a dying and a birth. The familiar life horizon has been outgrown; the old concepts, ideals, and emotional patterns no longer fit; the time for the passing of a threshold is at hand."

His early years proved to Joseph that he could do whatever he wanted to do without having to be a slave to money—one of the characteristics associated with those courageous enough to truly follow their bliss as he did. Living on very little, making himself easily available as a dinner guest, and free-lancing sometimes as a jazz musician, Joseph was able to spend

old emotional patterns

long periods of time simply reading—all the while mining the treasure trove of knowledge which later became available to us all through his prolific writing. "Follow your bliss" was an expression I heard him use often, and he practiced it faithfully in his own life. Once he said, "If you follow your bliss, you'll always have your bliss; but if you follow money, you may lose it at some time."

From his self-imposed exile in Woodstock, Joseph went on to teaching at Sarah Lawrence College in 1934—where he stayed until retiring as Professor Emeritus in 1972 and where he met his wife Jean Erdman, the noted dancer, choreographer, and artist in her own right. Along the way, he managed to assist the Vedanta Swami Nikhilananda in editing the thousand-page *The Gospel of Sri Ramakrishna* into English; he also edited the posthumous works of Heinrich Zimmer (whom Joe referred to as "my guru"), which included the classic text *Philosophies of India* and the massive two-volume masterwork *The Art of Indian Asia*. He also edited the multi-volume *Eranos Notebooks*, based on the Jung conferences in Zurich, for the Bollingen Foundation.

He then spent four years working on *The Hero with a Thousand Faces*, first published in 1949, and the history of sacred myths which was published as the monumental four-volume *The Masks of God*. Another four years was spent deciphering James Joyce's *Finnegans Wake* while writing his own *A Skeleton Key to Finnegans Wake*. He also edited *The Portable Jung* and *The Portable Arabian Nights*. In 1975, Princeton University Press published his *The Mythic Image* after ten years in preparation. I recall the flash in his eyes and his childlike glee and excitement about its publication, because it was one of those rare text and illustration/photo books where the words match the image you're seeing on the page instead of requiring you to refer to later pages explaining the visuals. The book is a veritable *tour de force* of the Campbell/Jung version of the unconscious, with powerful images evoking the deepest parts of ourselves. As Joseph once said, "The first function of a mythology is to waken and maintain in the individual a sense of wonder and participation in the mystery of this finally inscrutable universe." In 1983, *The Way of the Animal Powers*, the first volume of the *Historical Atlas of World Mythology*, was published. Certainly through his abundant writings, which will most assuredly remain in print throughout our lifetimes, and in his ebullient being, Joseph was a living example of his credo, fueled as he was by the magic and mystery of myth.

He had a young man's wonder about him. The quest was clearly where his fire burned brightest. I was always amazed by how open he was to new information. He was not rigid but still maintained a malleability of mind sufficient to allow growth to occur. A few years ago, telling me about his visit to the Picasso exhibition in New York City, he said: "This winter in New York the big thing for me was the Picasso exhibition, four miles of pictures by this man. At the age of sixteen, he produced two paintings which were of academic perfection. He had gotten into the academy by passing the exam when he was thirteen. So what do you do with your life if you're producing academically perfect works at the age of sixteen? Every step afterwards is an innovation. You see it visually as you go from one display room to the next. He was like the growing point, *actually* the growing point, of the whole twentieth-century pressure of Art into new regions. It's terrific!" Here you gain insight into Joe's openness to being re-inspired, not simply resting on his laurels but still questing after the Grail.

As I noted earlier, Joseph took pride in the fact that he never did anything primarily for money. This was because he derived so much fulfillment from doing just what was important to him, what was meaningful. He adeptly followed the Buddhist principle of "right living." Once, when I was speaking with him about his capacity to forgo the usual trappings of the materialistic mainstream, he replied by saying that he had luck; I thereupon asked, "Isn't there a myth that says you create your own luck?" Laughing loudly, he retorted, "That's not only myth!"

Joseph's life and work are an inspiration. I feel privileged and blessed to have known him. Those moments we shared together are special times I will always treasure. Now you, the reader, can share some of that illuminating experience through this selection of conversations. William Blake's words come to mind as I reflect on what I know of Joseph's extraordinary life: "Arise and drink your bliss! For everything that lives is holy." During his life, Joseph Campbell quaffed great gulps of bliss and his enormous contribution most assuredly points the way to what is holy.

MICHAEL TOMS
MENDOCINO COUNTY, CALIFORNIA
AUGUST 15, 1988

Arise and drink your bliss!
For everything that lives is holy!

—William Blake

MICHAEL: *We tend to use the word "myth" to mean something that is untrue or an erroneously held belief. Why is that?*

JOSEPH: I can understand why that idea arose. Myth is metaphor. The imagery of mythology is symbolic of spiritual powers within us: when these are interpreted as referring to historical or natural events which science in turn shows could not have occurred, then you throw the whole thing out. You see, myths do not come from a *concept* system; they come from a *life* system; they come out of a deeper center. We must not confuse mythology with ideology. Myths come from where the heart is, and where the experience is, even as the mind may wonder why people believe these things. The myth does not point to a fact; the myth points beyond facts to something that informs the fact.

When you think, for instance, "God is thy father," do you think he is? No, that's a metaphor, and the metaphor points to two ends: one is psychological—that's why the dream is metaphoric; the other is metaphysical. Now, dream is metaphoric of the structures in the psyche, and your dream will correspond to the level of psychological realization that you are operating on. The metaphysical, on the other hand, points past all conceptualizations, all things, to the ultimate depth. And when the two come together, when psyche and metaphysics meet, then you have a real myth. And when that happens the sociological and the cosmological aspects of your life have to be re-visioned in terms of these realizations.

So there are two stages to this: one is going inward, and finding the relationship of your own deepest self to the ground of being so that you become transparent to transcendence; the other is bringing this realization back into operation in the field, which is the work of the artist—to interpret the *contemporary* world as experienced in terms of relevance to our inner life.

To me, all mythologies are provinces of one great system of feeling. I think of the mythological image as an energy-evoking sign that hits you below the thinking system. Then words can be found to interpret the mythic image: image of the structure. Essentially, mythologies are enormous poems that are renditions of insights, giving some sense of the marvel, the miracle and wonder of life. And a poet working within a mythological system has the advantage of the major structuring images being already at hand. All he's giving is part of the big myth.

So that out of your search for understanding you create a myth.

No, I think it's not so much a search for understanding as it is sudden insight. You walk into a forest, you're not in quest of something. Suddenly you are struck by the wonder of this place. A woodpecker flies past: this tells you something about the wonder of the whole world of birds, of nature and so forth. And if you are a poet, you will attempt to render the quality of that experience insofar as it pushes right through to the ultimate mystery of being and life itself. That such a creature should be there! That the universe should be here! That's something that excites you to wonder.

We are mentally oriented in our period, so we always think it's a quest for interpretations. The theory that myths were attempts to answer questions about meaning was very popular at the end of the last century, and at the beginning of this one; but now we realize that these are great poems and that they don't represent answers but are attempts to express insights.

Now, in the older traditions, this was generally understood. One such symbolic theme, for example, is the virgin birth which occurs throughout American Indian mythology. This is what awakened me to the realization that these things had nothing to do with historical events. The mythic image of the virgin birth refers to the birth of the spiritual life in the human animal. We can live with the same interests as animals: clinging to life, begetting future generations, and winning our place in the world. But then there can open the sense of the spiritual quest and realization—the birth of the spiritual life. And this essentially is the virgin birth.

There are several elements in mythology: the Hero, for instance, and the Call. When did "the Call" first appear in mythology?

In mythology? That's the *essence* of mythology, I would say. The theme of the visionary quest; the one who goes to follow a vision. It appears one way or another in practically every mythology I know of.

So it's the core of all myth.

Yes, because the Hero is the one who has gone on the adventure and brought back the message, and who is the founder of institutions—and the giver of life and vitality to his community.

In the chapter of The Hero with a Thousand Faces *entitled "The Refusal of the Call," you talk about how we often follow society, and with the Call the reverse is what's more appropriate.*

There are two ways of living a mythologically grounded life. One way is just to live what I call "the way of the village compound," where you remain within the sphere of your people. That can be a very strong and powerful and noble life. There are, however, people who feel this isn't the whole story. And today, all historical circumstances are changing, and we no longer have the enclosing horizons that shut us in from knowledge of other people—new worlds are breaking in on us all the time. It's inevitable that a person with any sense of openness to new experience will say to himself, "Now, this won't do, the way we're living." Do you see what I mean? And so, one goes out for one's self to find a broader base, a broader relationship.

On the other hand, there's plenty of reason for those who don't have this feeling to remain within the field because our societies today are so rich in the gifts that they can render. But if a person has had the sense of the Call—the feeling that there's an adventure for him—and if he doesn't follow that, but remains in the society because it's safe and secure, then life dries up. And then he comes to that condition in late middle age: he's gotten to the top of the ladder, and found that it's against the wrong wall.

If you have the guts to follow the risk, however, life opens, opens, opens up all along the line. I'm not superstitious, but I do believe in spiritual magic, you might say. I feel that if one follows what I call one's "bliss"—the thing that really gets you deep in the gut and that you feel is your life—doors will open up. They do! They have in my life and they have in many lives that I know of.

There's a wonderful paper by Schopenhauer, called "An Apparent Intention of the Fate of the Individual," in which he points out that when you are at a certain age—the age I am now—and look back over your life, it seems to be almost as orderly as a composed novel. And just as in Dickens' novels, little accidental meetings and so forth turn out to be main features in the plot, so in your life. And what seem to have been mistakes at the time, turn out to be directive crises. And then he asks: "Who wrote this novel?"

Life seems as though it were planned; and there is something *in* us that's causing what you hear of as being accident prone: it's something in ourselves. There is a mystery here. Schopenhauer finally asks the question: Can anything happen to you for which you're not ready? I look back now on certain things that at the time seemed to me to be real disasters, but the results turned out to be the structuring of a really great aspect of my life and career. So what can you say?

And the other point is, if you follow your bliss, you'll have your bliss, whether you have money or not. If you follow money, you may lose the money, and then you don't have even that. The secure way is really the insecure way and the way in which the richness of the quest accumulates is the right way.

Joseph, in that same chapter on the Call, you wrote: "The myths and folk tales of the whole world make clear that the refusal [of the Call] is essentially a refusal to give up what one takes to be one's own interest." And then you go on to talk about how we get fixed in our own security and our own ideals and are reluctant to see them change.

Yes. And it can even get so that you can't make them change.

That brings up the whole connection of myth to the adventure. I'd like to hear you talk about that.

There's a kind of regular morphology and inevitable sequence of experiences if you start out to follow your adventure. I don't care whether it's in economics, in art, or just in play. There's the sense of the potential that opens out before you. And you have no idea how to achieve it; you start out into the dark. Then, strange little help-mates come along, frequently represented by little fairy spirits or the little gnomes, who just give you clues, and these open out. Then there is the sense of danger you always run into—really deep peril— because no one has gone this way before. And the winds blow, and you're in a forest of darkness very often and terror strikes you.

So often we see those dark places as huge problems rather than as opportunities. What does mythology have to say about that?

Well, mythology tells us that where you stumble, there your treasure is. There are so many examples. One that comes to mind is in *The Arabian Nights*. Someone is plowing a field, and his plow gets caught. He digs down to see what it is and discovers a ring of some kind. When he hoists the ring, he finds a cave with all of the jewels in it. And so it is in our own psyche; our psyche is the cave with all the jewels in it, and it's the fact that we're not letting their energies move us that brings us up short. The world is a match for us and we're a match for the world. And where it seems most challenging lies the greatest invitation to find deeper and greater powers in ourselves.

Toynbee speaks of challenge and response, and every culture and individual runs into these challenges. If the power to respond fails, then that's the end. But where the power to respond succeeds, there comes a new amplification of life and consciousness.

When I wrote about the Call forty years ago, I was writing out of what I had read. Now that I've lived it, I know it's correct. And that's how it turned out. I mean, it's valid. These mythic clues work.

What does the saying "Dread the passage of Jesus, for he does not return" mean to you in the context of what we've been talking about?

Jesus represents the inspiration to life, I mean the life of the spirit, not simply of physical conditions, but the thing that is life for man, namely the spiritual adventure. He comes and is the awakener; and if you close your mind to that awakener, he may not come back again. You can lose it. I think there are many myths, many epic stories, of the awakening which then passes and you can't even think what it was.

There's an extremely interesting psychological story of a woman in the hills of West Virginia who, when she was a little girl walking through the woods, heard wonderful music. And when she got home, she forgot what it was. Now, this is a woman in her late sixties who felt that she had missed her life, and it was only while in psychoanalysis that it came out that the song she had heard was the Call.

This, curiously, is precisely the problem of the shaman: the young person who is alone on the seashore or in the forest and hears music; those people who have the knowledge that the music must somehow be followed must stay with it. It may make a lonely life for you, but that is your life. And this to me was a very interesting theme. I'm sure that in our world, where emphasis is put on success and all that, the song is heard and forgotten by young people.

That's missing the Call. "Dread the passage of Jesus, for he may not return."

Does the Call only occur when you're young?

Oh, no! But it first occurs when you're young. Do you know that lovely poem by Wordsworth, *Intimations of Immortality?*

> "Our birth is but a sleep and a forgetting:
> The Soul that rises with us, our life's Star . . ."

And then he tells of the shades of the prison house beginning to close upon the growing boy, but he can still see the light in his joy. But it may yet be closed down.

On the other hand, if you stay open, you'll not only hear the song, but you'll hear it in great symphonic composition as you go on, so that you know that you're still on the track.

The other aspect of mythology that has always fascinated me, is the vision quest. What is the vision quest?

That is part of the basic myth. It is the quest to find the visionary relationship to the world. And as the world changes, the vision quest changes as well.

Now, the first visions were those of the shamans in the caves. But their people were just very small groups compared with the population now. When settled peoples began to increase, about the ninth millennium B.C., the problem of relating to those shamanic visions came up and the more complicated priestly relationships developed. Then the shaman is replaced by the priest, who represents the gods of the community. The shaman's deities were his own private familiars whom he discovered in vision; the deities of a larger social group are inherited by the tribe. And the priest is the officer of those deities. He doesn't necessarily experience them as the shaman does. Now, that poetic experience is what we've got to have again. It's much easier to have a poetic experience in the beautiful mountains and forests of California than it is to have the poetic experience in the factories of Detroit, but that's where it's got to be. To reactivate our world the vision quest has to deal with *our* world.

Another aspect of the vision quest is the encounter with demons.

Our demons are our own limitations, which shut us off from the realization of the ubiquity of the spirit. And as each of these demons is conquered in a vision quest, the consciousness of the quester is enlarged, and more of the world is encompassed. Basically the vision quest involves getting past your own limitations, which are within even as they appear to be without. They are symbolized in myth as monsters and demons, and in each age the characteristics change; because as a people changes, so do its limitations.

In some sense, our gods become our demons, don't they?

My definition of a devil is a god who has not been recognized. That is to say, it is a power in you to which you have not given expression, and you push it back. And then, like all repressed energy, it builds up and becomes completely dangerous to the position that you're trying to hold.

One of the best examples of that is the trickster figure in American Indian myth: the coyote, and the rabbit. He's at once a fool and a creator. He's a fool in that he's not acting in terms of the order of life in progress; and he's a creator in that he is the unrecognized, yet pressing energies that are threatening to break through.

One of the obsessions, I think, in Christianity is the Devil. When I turn from reading Oriental and tribal mythologies to any orthodox Christian work, suddenly the Devil is there. I think he's more important than God. He's the reason for all the wars against other people. He justifies the massacre of primitive tribes. They are all "Devil worshipers." Anyone who has an experience of the divine that's not of some particular clergy, is worshiping the Devil. And "Devil" is the word that's actually used for other people's gods.

I like that story about Padmasambhava, who went to Tibet and was faced with all of these demons, and evil deities of the Bon tradition. He basically transformed them into protectors of the dharma, *and that's exactly what we're talking about.*

That's an old mythological trick. The savior hero overcomes a demon and then makes him the protector. There's a wonderful story of the Buddha, two incarnations before his last, when he was Prince Five Weapons. As a young man, he had learned how to use five weapons. He's riding home now, a triumphant young warrior prince, when out of a forest comes a great big demon, a great monster, who's name is "Sticky Hair." The future Buddha is threatened by this monster, so he throws his javelin at him and it sticks in the monster's hair. Then he gets his bow and arrow and sends arrow after arrow at the monster, and they all stick in his hair. Then he throws his discus and it sticks in his hair. He takes his sword; it also sticks. He takes his club, and that, too, sticks in his hair. Then he hits him with his right fist, then his left; they stick. He kicks him with his right foot, then with his left; these also stick. Then Prince Five Weapons butts the monster with his head. Do you recognize this? This is Brer Rabbit with his Tar Baby. It's the same story. So he's stuck!

The demon says, "I'll bet you're frightened now, boy, huh?"

And Prince Five Weapons says, "No. I'm not, because I have within me a knowledge that will blow both of us to smithereens, and you're afraid of that. I'm not."

So the demon says, "Okay." And lets him loose.

The Buddha had conquered Sticky Hair. And then what did he do? He made him the guardian of that wood. It's giving due recognition to the monster; dealing with it, and then giving it its place. Its place might be the very same place it had all along, only you've now recognized that place and its importance. Do you see what I mean?

And the relevance to that in everyday life is that so often we tend to repress our demons and shove them into the background, push them into the closet and not deal with them.

And then they become the monsters.

And what could be the creative adventure becomes the journey through hell. Why do you think we continue to repress our demons and not deal with them?

Because they ask for a larger dimension in our lives than we're willing or able to give. I mean, it's important to hold a form and not just to explode. But in doing that, you should know what the powers are that are being asked to hold back, because recognizing them is part of integrating them. And the form that you're holding is held in relation to what it's not doing.

Say that again.

What?

[Michael laughs]: *Say the same thing differently. How's that?*

Well, I think you have to control your life; you can't let all of your impulse system take over. You wouldn't have a life. You'd go to pieces.

But in some sense, when you follow the adventure, you really have to let go of wanting to control it.

That's the problem. And that's why I say, "Heavy winds blow." There's a saying in one of the *Upanishads*, "The narrow blade of a razor is this: it's a narrow, difficult path." And the problem is that this is the real power of the left hand path of following your bliss instead of instructions. You're following the lead of your emotion and of your vitality; but the head has to be there all the time because you're on a narrow ridge and in danger of falling off. That is to say, letting too much of the torrent of energy come through will blow it.

There's nothing right or wrong when you're on the path, but there *is* imprudent and prudent action. Do you see what I mean? Because while you're beyond good and evil, as soon as you step out of the society, you can lose your life. Life is a dangerous path.

What is the counterpart of the vision quest in Christian mythology?

The mystical approach. What might be called the Pentecostal point of view: through your own inward experience, the divine mystery is revealed.

This is the wonderful thing about the American Indian tradition: that sense of a divine realization is possible to everyone, and one's whole life is based on the experience of that vision. Whether the young man was to become a great warrior or a shaman or a chieftain was revealed to him at that time. So you find your own way through experience—a way in the world in which you're living.

Why is it important to appreciate such a myth? And is it relevant to our times?

I think that for Americans, American Indian material is very important, because the mythology is rooted in the land as well as in the psyche. *Our* mythology has been brought from the Near East, a very long time ago, and it does not relate to our land unless we can, through our own experience, make it so. Do you see? And if you do not have that experience, then the Holy Land is somewhere else. But the great realization of mythology is the immanence of the divine—here and now— you don't have to go anywhere else for it. This *is* the holy land, the holy moment. And to find the Christ-power *here* is the goal of such a meditation.

Myth also informs us about the stage of life we're in. Isn't that so?

Yes. Actually, that's one of the main functions of myth. It's what I call the pedagogical: to carry a person through the inevitable stages of a lifetime. And these are the same today as they were in the paleolithic caves: as a youngster you're dependent on parents to teach you what life is, and what your relationship to other people has to be, and so forth; then you give up that dependence to become a self-responsible authority; and, finally, comes the stage of yielding: you realize that the world is in other hands. And the myth tells you what the values are in those stages in terms of the possibilities of your particular society.

Let's take a typical myth that most people would be familiar with: King Arthur and the Knights of the Round Table, and the search for the Holy Grail. How would that myth relate to the present?

There are about four quite distinct versions of the Grail quest. The earliest example we have is by Chrétien de Troyes, around 1190. But the most magnificent one is that of Wolfram von Eschenbach, about 1220. The best known version in the English language is that of a Cistercian monk whose name is lost to us. In that story, Galahad plays the main role.

Now the versions of Chrétien and Wolfram have a married man as the hero, who is a virtuous and competent warrior knight. On the other hand, the Cistercian quest which is called *La Queste del Saint Graal*, gives us the monkish figure, Galahad. For me, the great one is the quest of Parzival.

The problem of the grail quest is the re-vivification of what is known as the Waste Land. The Waste Land is a world where people live not out of their own initiative, but out of what they think they're supposed to do. People have inherited their official roles and positions; they haven't earned them. This is the situation of the Waste Land: everybody leading a false life. T. S. Eliot used that idea in his poem, *The Waste Land*, and he actually quotes several lines from Wolfram's *Parzival*. The Waste Land is a place where the sense of the vitality of life has gone. People take jobs because they have to live, and then they find in mid-life that the job doesn't mean a thing.

Now, the hero of the Grail is one who acts out of his own spontaneous nature. He comes to the Grail castle where the Grail king is maimed and lame, as the whole country is. Why is he maimed and lame? Because he just inherited the job. I won't go through how it all happened, but the sense of it is that he was not living out of the spontaneity of his own life. Unfortunately, when the hero of the Grail was told how to be a knight, he was told that knights do not ask questions. So when he sees the maimed king, he is moved to ask, "What ails you?" That is, the quality of compassion and sympathy moves him. But then he thinks, "A knight does not ask questions," and so he represses the impulse of his nature, and the quest fails. It takes him five or six more years to get back to the castle. But the spunk and pluck of his tenacity on the quest, and the revision of the mistake he made, yield the healing of the land.

So the meaning of the Grail and of most myths is finding the dynamic source in your life so that its trajectory is out of your own center and not something put on you by society. Then, of course, there is the problem of coordinating your well-being and your virtue with the goods and needs of the society. But first you must find your trajectory, and then comes the social coordination.

You once said that certain mythic heroes need never have existed in actuality, but are myths nevertheless. How could a myth just exist in its own right?

Well, I like to suggest that book of John Neihardt's, *Black Elk Speaks*. It's a perfect example of how a mythology can get born. Here was a boy only about nine years old, when he had this simply glorious vision, which Neihardt, as a great poet, was able to translate from the old medicine man's expression of it. It was a vision experienced in a sort of shamanic trance-state, and it came before the battle of Wounded Knee: that is to say, when the whole Indian world of our great West was really broken up. But what did the vision say? The vision said: "We have to change our center from a buffalo-oriented religion to a plant-oriented religion. Furthermore, the hoop of our little society has to be recognized among many other hoops." That was the prophetic insight that came. And that wonderful image of the transformation of the tree and the hoop among hoops—this is good stuff for today. A tribe that thought it was *It* is now in a multiple heterogeneous world. And this dear old man, when he was ninety or so, said: "I had a vision with which I might have saved my people, but I had not the strength to do it."

So what does he do with this vision?—and this is what is always done with prophetic visions of this kind—he teaches the people how to render it in a ritual activity. There's an interplay between the prophet and the people to whom he's talking. There is a dialogue between the great visionary and the people out of whom he has come. A myth originates from a poetical insight on somebody's part. He has experienced potentials that all of them might have experienced had they been poets.

Now, a ritual is the enactment of a myth: by participating in the rite, you participate in the myth. Myths don't count if they're just hitting your rational faculties—they have to hit the heart. You have to absorb them and adjust to them and make them your life. And insofar as the myth is a revelation of dimensions of your own spiritual potential, you are activating those dimensions in yourself and experiencing them.

When you find a poem or a picture that really appeals to you, and awakens you, there is someone who went ahead of you and gives you that experience; and it may be life-shaping. A myth is a life-shaping image.

Ritual, however, very soon becomes rote.

That's always the danger. But that's the danger, for example, in an art school. The work of the great master is imitated, and you have a series of imitations done with more or less skill.

How can we keep the poetry alive?

This is the whole problem of being alive, keeping your active imagination going. I know a lot of people who have done it. It's not something that just happens to you. If you spend all of your time thinking of economic problems, you're not going to spend enough time on your own inward imaginative world. You're not going to spend enough time on that to have anything really significant come of it. But you can participate in the visions of others: playing music, looking at pictures, going to museums.

The Olympics is another example of a ritual, isn't it?

Well, it started as a ritual in ancient Greece. And when you go to Delphi you really get the sense of the Greek ideal. At Delphi there was the Oracle, the unconscious, the depth speaking, telling you the truths. And there are the beautiful temples, and the theater. All these buildings were associated with religious experience. And at the top is the stadium where the events were held. And any young Greek who could run a good 180 yards was eligible to participate.

The ideal of the total man is a beautiful idea, and the Greeks represented it in a way that no other culture did. There were athletics in other traditional cultures but usually they were associated with the governing caste, or the warrior caste. But in Greece the idea of the total man held forth. I guess the Greeks were the first to have the Idea of Man, instead of man of a special race or a special career.

You mentioned the shaman in regard to the vision quest and Black Elk. Could you talk a little about the importance of the shaman and his role?

The medicine man was primarily one who'd had a profound psychological experience in adolescence—the shamanic crisis—what would be diagnosed today as a schizophrenic crackup. He has gone into the world of the unconscious and met its demons and deities. I mentioned the person walking on the seashore or in the forest, and he hears a strange music. This is the music of the spirits talking to him. A relationship is established, and he's got to hold on to that relationship; otherwise he loses his life. He is brought out of the crisis by the ministrations of an older shaman who gives him mythic instruction and the disciplines to function as a shaman. Now, the life of a shaman was a difficult one, of deep psychological responsibilities and experiences which he himself hardly understood. It was really a form of mystical experience of an accord with an aspect of nature. And with regard to that, his social position was one of isolation and of practices of his spiritual craft. He related to his society in certain specific ways: healing—that was his principal role—and conjuring the animals of the hunt into manifestation, knowing where they were, and other kinds of services. But he was typically feared. And the instrument of his song—the drum—was of tremendous power. The high statement of shamanism, as far as our anthropological information goes, was in Siberia. And the shaman's drum was of such a magical power that if the tribe were moving, the shaman with his drum would follow on a kind of sledge; no one could walk on the ground that the drum had passed over. The shaman's powers were great, and among the American Indians even today, shamanic practices are still effective.

The shaman is primarily associated with early hunting cultures. Later, in agriculturally based societies, he is in a secondary position.

There are in the caves in France—Lascaux and others—a number of representations of shamans in action.

Yes. The other source of our knowledge of the shaman is from the Siberian peoples, and the North American Indian tribes. The figure now in the primary role is the priest, who is an ordained official of the tribal or village deities; these are not of his personal experience. He is in the service of the society and its deities, for the priestly society. The shaman is an archaic danger. He represents the early mystic, one who has had the individual mystic experience and is supported by his familiars—his own special deities—whereas the priest is supported by and is in turn the supporter of the culture deities. The two systems are inherently in conflict. The priest is the man of the book; the shaman is the man of the experience. Of course, in the priestly culture there are also mystics who are the counterparts to the shaman. Now, with the insecurity that we feel regarding our religious institutions, there is a kind of drift to the shamanic idea.

Is the shaman in the realm of the Hero myth? Could a man like Castenada's Don Juan relate to a Quetzalcoatl, say, and become a myth that could be passed down?

Well, now, Quetzalcoatl, or Kukulcán in the Mayan formulation, is a high culture figure and he is intimately related to the observations that were made on the cycles of the planet Venus. His disappearances and reappearances and their timing, as well as the legends associated with them, are geared right in to the cycle of the planet Venus in relation to the cycles of the sun and the moon, and to the artificial cycle of thirteen times twenty days of the Mayan-Aztec calendars. So, for a figure like Don Juan ever to be translated into that context would require a high-culture absorption of the figure. Now, the whole question of Quetzalcoatl is an interesting one because the figure certainly is mythological; and yet there was also a historical character by that name, who is important in the history of Yucatan. No doubt the historical character was named after the mythic character and then the two became contaminated in our received traditions. It's as though a person were named Jesus, as many a Spaniard or Mexican is, and that person's life story got mixed up with the story of Jesus of Nazareth, you see? I think something like that has happened in the handing down of the legends associated with Quetzalcoatl. Now, if a person like Don Juan had initiated some historical event of momentous significance, he might become assimilated to a Quetzalcoatl idea. But that model derives from a cosmological observation.

Don Juan does fit other aspects of the Hero myth.

Oh, it's a Hero myth. No doubt about it. But there are different kinds of Hero myths. Any visionary can become a figure of a Hero myth, as does Moses when he goes up on the mountain and envisions the Word and comes back with it. That's the Hero deed of going in quest of the Word and coming back and delivering the Word.

There are many Navaho legends in which people go off into the fields or mountains, following the call of a mountain goat or something, have some illumination, and then come back with a teaching. Black Elk is a Hero figure. But he did not himself associate with a cosmological principle.

It has to have a more universal application?

Yes. Exactly that. Now, the historical character of Jesus is assimilated into Christianity through the theological Person— that is, the second Person in the Blessed Trinity, who's not a historical character but is antecedent to time. The crux of Christianity is the identification of that historical character as the only incarnation in history of the second Person of the Blessed Trinity. The second Person in the Blessed Trinity is a theological principle. When Paul says, "I live now not I, but Christ in me," he didn't say Jesus, the historical character, in me, he said "Christ in me."

Let me ask you about another matter. What about the role of the fool?

Well, again in primitive hunting cultures, that's the trickster hero. Almost all non-literate mythology has a trickster hero of some kind. American Indians had the great rabbit and coyote, the ravens, and blue jay. And there's a very special property in the trickster: he always breaks in, just as the unconscious does, to trip up the rational situation. He's both a fool and someone who's beyond the system. And the trickster hero represents all those possibilities of life that your mind hasn't decided it wants to deal with. The mind structures a lifestyle, and the fool or trickster represents another whole range of possibilities. He doesn't respect the values that you've set up for yourself, and smashes them.

The fool really became the instructor of kings because he was careless of the king's opinion, careless of the king's power; and the king allowed this because he got wisdom from this uncontrolled source. The fool is the breakthrough of the absolute into the field of controlled social orders.

To some extent, we've lost our court jesters.

Some of our journalists are real court jesters, I think. And at the end of the Tarot cards is the Fool, the one who's gone through all the stages that are represented in that series of cards, and now can wander through the world, careless and fearful of nothing.

From your knowledge of mythology and the ancient past, is it possible that other civilizations, greater than our own, once flourished on the earth and have totally disappeared?

It would be hard to know where they would have been. Civilization, as we usually think of the term, involves monumental architecture, writing, and mathematical systems— things of that sort. These all come in as a constellation about 3500 B.C. in Mesopotamia. The next great jump is in Egypt itself, which then becomes one of the most majestic civilizations ever because it was relatively protected. And for 4,000 years, there it was, right up to the time of the Theodosian Code in the fourth century A.D.

China during the Shang Dynasty [c. 1523 B.C.] is not a high civilization; it's neolithic, with planting and ceramic ware, but not what we would call a civilization. And we know that Indian civilization starts about 2500 B.C. in the Indus Valley. And that's fairly well documented all the way down.

Then you jump to the Americas. The Olmec culture suddenly appears about 1100 B.C. And where in heaven's name would the others be? One talks about Lemuria and Atlantis, but the whole Lemurian situation is infinitely before the appearance of man on earth. You have to have some regard for geology! And as for Atlantis: I don't know what to say about that. There's no geologist who stands by it. The Atlantis legend which occurs in the *Timaeus* and the *Critias* of Plato has now been rather convincingly associated with that wonderful island in the Aegean, Thera, which really exploded about 1485 B.C. That's the period of the whole cycle of mother goddess legends, the world of old Europe, of which Marija Gimbutas has written in *The Gods and Goddesses of Old Europe*, 6500 to 3500 B.C. That is the period when the Miocene patriarchal system came over, just at the time the Hebrews were invading Canaan, and also bringing in a father-god. So, there certainly was a turnover in the mythological thinking of mankind about that time, moving from the mother-goddess to the father-god. But we know those earlier systems flourished. And we don't have to hypothesize an island in the Atlantic.

When the Atlantis legend was translated into modern thinking out of Plato, it still was thought—this was in the early nineteenth century—that the Mayan period was close in time to the Egyptian; but it wasn't.

Are the pyramids of South America the result of diffusion?

Yes.

Do you believe that the Mayans came from Atlantis and went to Egypt?

No!

The movement, then, is definitely from East to West.

That's the way the evidence points, it seems to me. Now, Hyerdal came across from the Egyptian realm, and we may find there was diffusion across the Atlantic from Egypt. But then why so late? The Egyptian pyramids date from about 2500 B.C., and the Mayan pyramids date from about 500 A.D. There's a little difference of 3,000 years. So where were these people all that time? Floating around somewhere? Did they get lost somewhere on the Island Inaccessible, in the middle of the Atlantic Ocean and then push off again 3,000 years later? There's got to be another explanation, I think. At least it doesn't convince me at all. The whole Atlantis-in-the-middle-of-the-Atlantic theory has trouble. When those theories were first proposed, at the end of the nineteenth century, these things weren't properly understood, and it was thought that people went eastward and westward and built pyramids. But you can't do that now. It seems to me the people who hold to this kind of thought are very, very slipshod about dates; and dates are kind of a mania for me.

So you're saying that the Yucatan pyramids couldn't have come from Egypt because of the 3,000-year gap.

Yes. And I am saying they did come from China and that area where there are temple pyramids which are not the same as the Egyptian pyramids. The Egyptian pyramids are pointed on top. The pyramids of Mesopotamia have a stairway, and a temple on top. And that's the kind of temple you have in the Mayan-Aztec zone. That's also the kind of temple you have in India, and in Southeast Asia. In the Aztec and Mayan ruins you have the same, modified by the material they used, of course. But the analogy is not with the Egyptian temple.

Perhaps a psychological significance could be attached to that common form.

You have to ask why people would want a temple like that. Why a great tower with a temple on top? It's because it represents a mythological concept of the cosmos. The idea is that the cosmos is a great mountain, with stages of worlds on the way up, the ultimate personification of the divine power being in that realm on the summit. It's with Mesopotamia to the Mayan-Aztec world that we have the closest analogues. Along with that comes astronomy: different powers located in the same planets. Likewise, mathematics is based on a 20 system here, on a 60 system over there, on a 10 over there, and so forth. Reading Morley's *The Ancient Maya* years ago, I noted the motifs from the Maya that parallel the Eastern traditions, and I filled three pages!

These seem to be universal truths which are bound to crop up in different places, each to find its own expression.

To speak for diffusion doesn't diminish the force of the psyche. Why does it last? It lasts because it has a symbolic meaning. It excites a resonance in the psyche, and a truth is somehow suggested.

A pyramid and a temple are more obvious, perhaps, than a piece of pottery.

Now, pottery is one of the most telling clues of diffusion because they can even analyze the glazes, the motifs, and the forms. There's a kind of pottery vessel, for example, that appears in China which stands on three legs; and the legs have the shape of a woman's breast, and they're standing on the nipples. Those occur in Mexico also. Now, that's a bizarre notion!

One of the big finds that I've reproduced in *The Mythic Image* is of a figure from Georgia seated in lotus position; not only in lotus position, but with the right hand in the boon-bestowing posture and the mouth slightly open in a kind of ecstasis. And right in the same culture context is a hand in a boon-bestowing posture with an eye in the palm, just as in the Bodhisattva Avalokiteshvara, and it's surrounded by serpent forms. Of course they're rattlesnakes here, because that's the great sacred serpent. But what are you going to do with this?

Are you saying, then, that the Mayans came at just a certain point from China?

I wouldn't want to put the whole thing that way and say that the Mayans came from China. But what I am saying is that the motifs of their iconography *do* match, in many essential ways, those of the high Far Eastern culture complexes, which include Indian material. There is very strong convincing evidence of trans-Pacific influences, dating from as early as 3000 B.C., and Robert Heine-Geldern actually gave a schedule of dates which I reproduced in *The Mythic Image*. Now, of course, when there is an outside influence, it's developed in the receiving area and it requires new stylistic inflections, as well as new things from the animal and vegetable world round about. And so there is great creative development.

To say that the motifs couldn't have come from the East, I think, is very hard. It's miraculous either way you read it actually; but my guess is for diffusion.

When I started *The Masks of God* years ago, I promised myself that I would not make a decision; I was just going to present the evidence and not load it with my own judgment. But the more I worked on it, the more I found myself thinking: "This has come across the water." And how it came, I cannot say; nobody can. Now, you mentioned pottery. About ten years ago, pottery was discovered on the coast of Ecuador—the Valdivia pottery—which matched perfectly Middle Joman pottery from Kyushu, Japan, 3000 B.C. And in the publication from the Smithsonian Institution, you can't tell the difference between Middle Joman and Valdivia pottery when the two are presented on one page.

When this Japanese pottery was found in Ecuador, the first explanation offered was that a Japanese sampan or something of the kind got lost on the ocean, and there is an actual Pacific current that runs from Kyushu to the north of Hawaii and comes down to Ecuador. But does a boat of fishermen carry potters in it, so that within a few decades the pottery on this side is even more efficiently done than the pottery on that side? That just won't hold water. You've got to have some kind of significant expedition or adventure. As one scholar said in answer to critics, "If this doesn't prove diffusion, let's stop talking about pottery."

And then there is the hero called Tunapa or Tanupa, the one who resembles Christ? According to stories, he walked through the Andes carrying a wooden cross, had disciples, and talked to people about morality. Eventually he was run off or killed. Is that a case of diffusion also?

I don't know of that particular hero. I do know of a couple of pictures, in some of the Aztec works which are pre-Columbian, that show a figure carrying a cross. Furthermore a cross is associated with Quetzalcoatl and Kukulcán. But the cross is a basic symbol for the world and the center: the four points of the compass, and the fifth point is in the middle, which is the transcendent point. And of course the savior figure is the one who transcends the pairs of opposites and is associated with the center. So, such a figure carrying a cross is striking as an analogue *Via Crucis* of Jesus. It's not something that would *have* to have been brought over by the Spaniards at all.

Wouldn't the cross tend to be of equal proportions?

It would tend to be that. But the picture I have in mind, and which is also reproduced in *The Mythic Image*, is of a cross with one end a little longer than the other.

Curious; it doesn't seem to fit the symbolism.

No, it doesn't, but that's the way it is. It may have had something to do with the tradition, but we don't know what the tradition associated with this figure was.

And in Palenque there is the Temple of the Cross. That temple must date from before 900 A.D. Because that area was abandoned by that time; the whole culture moved out to Yucatan. So this can't have been brought over by the Christians. There it is: the Temple of the Cross. There are two figures, one on either side of that temple. And as I say, the cross is associated with Kukulcán and Quetzalcoatl. Not only is Quetzalcoatl associated with the cross, but you have a virgin birth, a departure, a second coming; you've got the works! All associated with this hero, who's a major figure in the Mexican tradition.

There is a figure buried in the tomb of the Temple of Inscriptions. Do you have any idea who this was?

No. It could be a chieftain, a great priest; it could be a figure who was deified. Deification is easy in most cultures. The power that's represented in the deity is transferred to an individual. For instance, some of those who were sacrificed by the Aztecs were consecrated as deities and lived for a year as the deity, and then were slain, themselves believing in the tradition—because we are all gods, really, only we don't know it. And when the tradition deifies someone it simply says, "Let us regard in this person that which is true in all of us, but which we don't consider in our trade and political life"—namely, the immanence of the divine in the forms of the world.

Was it the Incas who foretold of men coming from the East with long beards and white faces?

I think that was an Aztec story. And Cortez happened to arrive right on the button, which is why he had a comparatively easy time to begin with. Of course, you can't underestimate the heroism of that act of Cortez's. It was a brutal, ruthless thing, but those men had guts. What was it—about forty men, overthrew a major empire. Of course, they had guns and horses—things that were startling to people. Then there was Pizarro, who was ruthless, entering the whole world of the Incas, driving all the way to the cities up there with no idea what he would meet; he just rode right into the main capitals.

The element of fear or of the unknown gave them the advantage?

Just imagine, you have a legend of the god from the East. The East is usually white—it's the color of dawn. Cortez arrives on a certain date, and he has gun power, explosives, and horses. Nobody there had ever seen men on horses before. And for a while they thought man and horse were one creature; they believed these were divine apparitions of a strange sort. So there was the shock effect, and from the Aztec point of view it was all pretty convincing stuff. But the fact that Cortez went on to overthrow that empire is just something fantastic. They had to tear down Tenochtitlán house by house to take it.

So their mythology prepared them for that defeat.

Well, I was just trying to say that I thought it was significant in that they thought it was the deity who came, and that delayed their realistic response to the assault. If they thought it was a deity, they did so because of the mythology they had and the mythology blinded them to what was actually going on.

How did it happen that in two parts of the continent—the Incas in the south and the Aztecs to the north—the mythology was so similar as to leave both civilizations vulnerable?

Merely that the two societies, which were very close to each other in time and place, had analogous myths.

Why was that, would you say?

Why do we have the idea of Christ's coming as a second coming? This is a standard motif in mythology: the one who has died is coming back. King Arthur wanted to come back, too, and I think probably Hiawatha as well.

That isn't what's surprising to me; or that the one from the East should be white. But I must say the coincidence of a person who fitted the description actually arriving, that's the fantastic thing. You can interpret that as you like, either as sheer coincidence or as a kind of prophetic foresight—or what Jung called "synchronicity." The mythological analogue, in the light of all that we know about motifs running through systems, isn't so surprising. The big surprise is that it matched what actually occurred.

There's similarity that runs from South America to North America. Take Viracocha and Quetzalcoatl, for example. Do you have any reason to believe they might have been the same being?

It's an equivalent archetype, and I've made the distinction between the elementary idea or archetype and the expression of the elementary idea or archetype through the patterns and traditions of separate people. Those are the folk ideas. And in that sense, Viracocha and Kukulcán or Quetzalcoatl are of the same archetype essentially. But in one case it appears in tradition A, and in the other case in tradition B, with the historical and local provincial circumstances determining the inflection of the form, the actual application, and the mythic circumstances in which the figure appears. That's what happens everywhere. Take, for instance, the trickster hero. Wotan has a trickster motif. There are tricksters in Polynesia. The trickster in the American plains is the coyote; in the northeast it's the rabbit. And in a part of Southeast Asia it's a tiny little deer. Now the big question is: "Do these arise in parallel independent ways, or is there actual diffusion to be recognized?" And of course, it will differ from case to case.

In some cases you can actually see the diffusion. For instance, the figure of Tammuz in Mesopotamia and Syria comes to Egypt as Osiris, and there's almost no doubt about it, whereas it's a little more difficult to connect Tammuz, say, with Quetzalcoatl. Do you see what I'm saying?

Yes. This gets back to what you said earlier about myths existing in the absence of an actual hero.

Yes. There's a whole theory about mythology that's called the Euhemeristic theory. There was a classical mythographer named Euhemerus in the fourth century B.C., shortly following the time of Alexander the Great. And he noticed that Alexander, within a hundred years, had become deified in the Near Eastern zone. So he drew the conclusion that deities were amplified human beings. And this is the Euhemeristic theory. But the important thing, from my standpoint, is not that a man has become deified, but the formula of deification: why is it that when a figure becomes deified here, the same thing happens to him as to the man who is deified over there? What is the psychological principle that deifies? And what are the rules and forms that it follows in action?

The same attributes are imposed.

That's what's interesting; that's the mythologization of an entity. But even if there's no entity there, that mythological motif could come in a dream, and then the dream becomes historicized. So, in such a case, it happens in the opposite direction; it works both ways.

So is there a common symbology?

There is.

And that would account for the same attributes . . .

Right. But if you find chariots, let's say, in a Chinese tradition, you'd know that the chariot came to China from southeast Europe. That would be an example of diffusion. The chariot wasn't invented independently in those two places, and when the deity is seen riding a chariot, we can say that this was carried over from one culture to the other.

Now, the whole South American and Mexican tradition has its roots in the period of the Olmec and Chavín cultures, which date from about 1200 and 800 B.C., respectively. The Olmec culture starts around 1200 suddenly. The antecedents are not to be located in the area around about, at least as far as I know. The Chavín seems to be about 300 years later, but related. The sort of jaguar face motif occurs in both, and you find it, of course, in China. In *The Mythic Image*, I've gone into this in considerable detail in a chapter about the cosmology of the New World. And I've indicated there what I do believe, namely, that the proposed evidence for influences from China, Northern Vietnam, and Cambodia of trans-Pacific diffusion of culture traits is *there*. That's all. So, we have a diffusion.

It's not attributable to the collective unconscious?

No, this is diffusion. If you have one motif here, and the same element there, well then, perhaps, yes. But if you have a constellation of about fifteen or twenty elements, or the whole range of the culture context—ideas, myths, actual details of costume, things like that—what are you going to do?

What is the relationship between the collective unconscious and mythology?

Mythology is an expression of the collective unconscious. I mean, you can define it that way. And I think that the Western interest in meditation which began in the 1960s, as well as the discoveries by young people of their own source land of mythology, led to the recognition that the real echo of all this was actually in Jung.

Now, my own discovery of Jung happened when I was a student in Germany in the 1920s. I was interested in mythology at that time. But I had never found any relationship of psychology to mythology in the literature that I was introduced to in college or graduate school. But, my god, when I began reading Jung's works—particularly the work that's been translated as *Symbols of Transformation*! That was just one of those things that sends all the lights up in all directions! I knew that a whole new dimension of understanding of what mythology was all about had come to me. So as far as the psychological interpretation of mythology and elucidation and evaluation go, I find Jung the base. Others who interest me now also relate to him positively: Stanislav Grof, and R.D. Laing.

Perhaps the reason Jung is accessible these days, is because many have used mind-altering substances and are searching for symbols and things that are inexpressible intellectually.

I think that's likely.

Is that why Stanislav Grof is so connected with him, too?

Oh, definitely! I think the psychology of Freud tends more to relate to what Jung calls the personal unconscious. When you break past that into realms that cannot be interpreted in terms of personal experience, you're in the field of mythic forms. And if you're acquainted with the mythic forms, you understand where you are in a way that's impossible if you have no previous acquaintanceship.

When you get down into the depths of mythology, forms are beyond good and evil. With the Indian deities—this is the wonderful thing about them—the upper right hand will say, "Fear not" and below it is the boon-bestowing hand; and the upper left will have a sword, and in the lower a recently amputated head. These are the two aspects of power, the two aspects of being. In our traditions—and this is true even all the way back to the Greeks—the beneficent and the malfeasant aspects of power tend to be separated and contrary entities.

Is that when trouble arises?

No, not necessarily—provided the two are in play with each other. But when one is impugned, as in our tradition where the powers of the deep are consigned to Hell . . . It's interesting that the symbols of Shiva and of Poseidon are exactly those that are given to the Devil in Christian mythology—the bull's foot and the tridents. So the power which is symbolized in those forms has been pushed aside as though it should not be admitted.

In Greece, however, the two do play against each other. For instance, Apollo and Dionysus. Dionysus is that bull and serpent power playing in concord with Apollo as the contrary figure. Nietzsche's *The Birth of Tragedy* is a key book to this whole thing.

Now, where I am separated from Jung is in my interest in the historical development of mythology—what Bastian called the folk transformations of the great archetypes which occur in the different provinces of human life. That was what I dealt with in *The Masks of God*.

The similarities and variations.

Yes. And the accents given in various cultures to the forms. For instance, a primitive hunting culture will have a totally different emphasis from a culture that is a planting or gathering culture. In the hunting culture, the food is generally brought in by the men and they have the prestige; whereas in the early planting and collecting cultures, the women are dominant, and you get another mythological context.

Also, if you're in a realm such as the great animal plains of Siberia, Northern Europe, and North America, you have a horizon that is a perfectly defined circle with the great dome of the sky over it. But if you are in the jungle lands of Brazil, Africa, or India, there is no sky and there is no horizon— you've got another world. Above you are the leafy treetops with singing birds; beneath is the leafy undergrowth with scorpions and serpents. So you not only have the female figure with vegetation all about—rotting vegetation and fresh vegetation coming up from the land—but you also have no horizon. Quite a different environment.

Have you found that situation more compatible to a matriarchal society?

Well, I wouldn't say "matriarchal." But it's a society in which the mother goddess principle—the earth principle—is dominant. Power is sought from the plant world. Whereas in the hunting societies, you'll find a god principle—the thunder-hurler or the solar light—as male, and the shamans will be moving upward, and the myths will tell of excursions into the upper sphere or beyond the horizon.

One final question. You've been talking about mythology in terms of guidelines. But does myth provide answers?

Only insofar as it points to certain commonalities. The main drift of mythology, if you want to put it into a sentence or two, is that the separateness that is apparent in the phenomenal world is secondary; beyond, and behind, and within, and supporting that world is an unseen but experienced unity and identity in us all. And the first level of unity that is recognized is that of the family. And the second level of unity, which is deeper, is of the tribe or the social unit. But beyond that is a common human identity.

There's another wonderful question Schopenhauer asked: How is it that an individual can so participate in the danger and pain of another that, forgetting his own self-protection, he moves spontaneously to the other's rescue, even at the cost of his own life? Schopenhauer's answer is that a metaphysical realization is showing its force in action, namely, the realization that you and that other are one, and that the sense of separateness is simply a function of the way we experience things in space and time.

Now, that spontaneous compassion, I think, would jump culture lines. If you were to see someone of a totally alien world—even a person of a race or nation that you had no sympathy for—the recognition of a common human identity would spark a response. And the ultimate reference of mythology is to that single entity, which is the human being as human.

So we almost have to go beyond rational thought to catch that connection.

This is *irrational.* That's the point. All compassion, all sympathy, is irrational. Love is irrational. The rational is always stressing *I-thou* opposites. The mind is in the world of separateness and angular structures. It's a world put together in a way that can be calculated. Compassion, love—these jump mathematics.

Perhaps the nature of conflict is related to the inability to go beyond the mind, to recognize the connection that we all have.

That's right. But then the opposite problem comes up: becoming too strongly linked to the commonalty—losing touch with your own individuality. Part of our loyalty to life is being loyal to our own lives, you see, not sacrificing your self, but letting oneself play in relation to the other in a prudent and positive way.

Striking a balance.

Exactly that. Striking a balance.

CHAPTER TWO

*M*ICHAEL: *Human beings throughout history have been searching for their source. How do you see today's search?*

*J*OSEPH: I think our search is somewhat encumbered by our concept of God. God as a final term is a personality in our tradition, so that breaking past that "personality" into the transpersonal, whether within one's self or in conceiving of the form beyond forms—although one can't even say form—is blocked by our orthodox training. This is so drummed into us, that the word "God" refers to a personality. Now, there have been very important mystics who have broken past that. For instance, there is Meister Eckhart, whose line I like to quote: "The ultimate leave-taking is the leaving of God for God." This is what in Sanskrit is so easily expressed in Saguna and Nirguna Brahman—Brahman with qualities and Brahman without qualities. And when people would go to Ramakrishna, he would ask them how they would like to talk about God, with qualities or without? You see, that's inherent in their tradition, but it's blocked in ours.

Has this changed recently?

This is exactly what I do begin to sense, because of the influence of Oriental teachers and teachings on people here. In our Oriental departments in universities we have magnificent scholars who can interpret Vedic and Sanskrit material, Buddhist or Hindu. They really know what they're talking about. And in those scholars' writings we're beginning to experience, even on the popular level, this concept of "the God beyond God."

Many people seem to be coming to the search for God.

Well, that's the great thing about it. As soon as you smash the local provincial god-form, God comes back. And that's what Nietzsche meant when he wrote that God is dead. Nietzsche was himself not an atheist in the crude sense; he was a man of enormous religious spirit and power. What he meant was that the God who's fixed and defined in terms appropriate for 2,000 years ago is no longer so today. And of course the words of Meister Eckhart give an earlier variation of Nietzsche's remark. So the concept of God beyond God is in our tradition.

Another example is the *Divine Comedy*. In those last stanzas of the last canto, Dante beholds the beatific vision, and behind it three great radiant rings of fire, and he tries to see how the personality aspect coincides with the abstract fire. He says, "This was beyond my comprehension until with the sudden illumination I was given the grace to know." And in that he saw that the whole world is a manifestation of God's love, including the fires of hell.

And here again is the combination of good and evil. There really is no difference, is there? Certainly the Buddhist view has been that there is no difference between Nirvana and Samsara.

The great thing—Yoga and Samsara are one, that's the sense of nondual realization. You go past the pairs of opposites and that, ultimately, on a sort of ABC level, is the difference between Hinayana [Buddhism] and Mahayana [Buddhism].

The Hinayana monastic way, where you leave the world of Samsara and the vortex of rebirth, is transcended when Nirvanic realization is achieved and you realize you are beyond the pairs of opposites so that this is Nirvana *here*. The Nirvanic revelation is of the way of experiencing what's here now so that it's radiant of the Mother Light.

Now, we get that in the wonderful *Gospel According to Thomas*, which has been translated from the Nag-Hammadi finds, where the very last passage opens the whole thing. Jesus says, "This generation will not pass away but these things will have come to pass." To interpret that as an end of the world is to misread the symbol. But that's the way it has been read. And of course, the world didn't pass away. This is what's called the great non-event: it didn't occur. My point is that to interpret symbolic forms as though they were references not to potentialities within the human spirit, but to historical events, is to misread them.

We have religions that are based on that passage in the Bible.

I know it! And the whole idea of the Second Coming is thought to be a historical event, too. Well, at the end of the Thomas Gospel, the disciples ask, "When will the kingdom come?" And Jesus answers, "The kingdom will not come by *expectation*. The kingdom of the Father *is* spread over the earth and men do not see it." In other words, bring it about in your hearts. And that is precisely the sense of Nirvanic realization. This is it. All you have to do is see it. And the function of meditation leading to that is to dissociate you from your commitment to this body, which is afraid to die, so that you realize the eternal dimension is right here, now, everywhere. And suffering and joy, good and evil are functions of the apparitional situation as things seem, but the ultimate is transcendence. This is right in the gospels, when Jesus says, "Judge not that you may not be judged" [Matthew 7:1] and "Be as your father in heaven whose rain falls on the just and the unjust." [paraphrase of Matthew 5: 45–48] But we, in our religions, have made a terrific point of ethical judgment. It's a fantastic distortion: historical and ethical references instead of the metaphysical. That doesn't mean that in your social life you shouldn't make ethical judgments, but they're not the mystery dimension of our potentials for experience.

Discrimination rather than judgment.

You're playing against people, and they're against you. Well, that's the game. It wouldn't be a tennis game if there weren't two sides of the net. But the umpire lets the rain fall on both sides. And we function in the world in two senses: in one sense as the viewer, including ourselves in the field, and in the other sense as actor. The actor has to act in terms of pairs of opposites. And the viewer has to view.

There's a little verse from the *Rig Veda* that I'm very much attached to, of the tree of life and two birds—fast friends. One eats the fruit of the tree and the other watches. Those are two aspects of ourselves: we eat the fruit—we kill a life in order to eat, and we play in the world of action. But then in contemplation, as the meditative one, we are removed from that world and its destiny. Those are two positions: the general which looks at the duality of life; and the particular which involves participation—the sorrows of life. There's a Buddhist formula of the Bodhisattva for the one who has illumination but who determines to remain in the world: all life is sorrowful. So the Bodhisattva participates with joy in the sorrows of the world. This is the crucified one. The Crucifixion is not something that should not have happened; that's something that *must* happen. It's an important concept.

This concept of "God within," is it common to ancient mythologies or did they always involve the Hero and God without?

Well, it's hard to know what people thought in periods that antedate the events of writing. You have to imagine on the basis of what you see. I would not be in a position to answer that question. The Navaho, for instance, have the idea of the fire that's in the sun being the fire in the heart, shining in the eyes. Both fires are one. That's what you get in the Egyptian idea of the dead person's becoming Osiris on the way to Osiris: to be one with that which he has been identical with all his life, though ignorant of the fact.

A merging.

Yes. There are different ways of imagining this which is ultimately not imaginable. Some of them sound as though they were becoming identical, and others sound as though they were realizing the identity but remaining separate. But the sense of it is that which is there—is the life by heart. When Saint Paul says, "I live now not I, but Christ in me," he's very close to that thought. The life of his life is the Christ.

In The Mythic Image, *Christ has the image of the Hero. How did it get lost in the first place; where did God and Christ separate from man?*

Those are big questions, and I'll try to answer them in two stages. First, the idea of a figure representing the fulfillment of man's spiritual potentials is one that appears in all of the very high religions. By "high religion," I mean a religion that is based on a literate base: it flourishes in a world of literacy. When you move to the non-literate traditions, you are on another scale and another set of images begins to come through. But the literate cultures are all historically related to each other.

We know when and where writing was invented. It was in 3200 B.C. in ancient Sumer and from there, with the concept of a high civilization—with professional priests, professional governors, professional trading people, professional artisans, professional planting and agricultural people—it goes in slow stages eastwards and westwards to the bounds of the world. And so, there is a continuity, and all the religions that grow from that basis are related. But they are inflected to the concerns of certain local culture worlds. One will be a world that is engaged principally in sea voyaging. Just think of the Greeks and the Aegean. Another is deeply inland, such as most of India—there's not much sea in their world. China: deserts to the west, ocean to the east—it's an isolated world there.

Myths take into their domain the conditions and even the geographical idiosyncrasies of the various landscapes. One will be in a desert land, another in a jungle, and so on. But at the base of the myths is a common vocabulary of images.

The myth of the great savior, for example, represents the culmination or fulfillment of human potentiality. In the Hindu and Buddhist systems, the point is made that this potential is within all of us. And we are all to become fulfilled in that sense. In the Christian system, however, the accent was put on one savior.

Then comes the question of why in the West there is only one incarnation of this potential. It's a complicated historical question concerning the first four centuries A.D. in the world of Byzantium. What finally happened was that Theodosius I (378–395, approximately) proclaimed Christianity to be the only religion permitted within the Roman Empire, and only the Augustinian interpretation of the doctrines was accepted. So you have a system set up principally by a small group of theologians, and this becomes enforced to the advantage of the institution. The individual is taught to find his salvation through the medium of the institution. And there is a whole interpretation of the life of the savior, which gives authority to this institution.

The interesting thing is that when you read the life of the saviors—Jain saviors, Buddhist saviors, Hindu saviors, the Christ—the same motifs are there, time and time and time again.

Turn to the wonderful Greek mystery religions, and again there are virgin births, death and resurrection. And the savior's death and resurrection becomes a model for the casting off of the old Adam and the un-shelling of the new. These are great, great themes.

In our Christian tradition, however, they have been carried in such a way that in order to get the grace, you might say, one has to approach the theme through the doctrines and the sacraments of the Church—that's the important thing. Man is born in Original Sin; the only salvation is through the sacraments of the Church. Now, that's fixing it down pretty fast. I find this has dislocated many young people. In my own teaching career I saw that when students found the analogues of their Christian or Jewish beliefs in other traditions, it actually reinforced their Christian and Jewish symbols, because now they saw how they had psychological value to them. Do you see what I mean?

What brought about my writing of *The Mythic Image* was the realization that mythology is basically pictorial and the language elucidates the pictures or communicates a story of pictorial transformations. When you compare the pictorial formulae of the great traditions, you find many analogues. One of them is that of the emergence of the savior figure from the womb of space, as though the divine broke through into our world by way of the goddess Space. And we find, in many traditions, the savior figure breaking through, surrounded by the zodiac—the zodiac would represent the limits of space. We have the savior Aion of Alexandrian Egypt; we have it in Mithraism; and we have it in the Christ. Now, the four figures that appear in the west portal of the cathedral at Chartres, representing the four evangelists—the bull, the lion, the eagle, and the man—are representative forms of four signs of the zodiac. And these four signs, in the fourth millennium B.C., were the signs of spring, mid-summer, autumn, and winter: the bull of spring, the lion of mid-summer, the eagle of fall, and the man—the water-carrier—of mid-winter. So Jesus coming through in a mandala which represents the organ of birth, with the four evangelists around him, is the birth through the world of space, representative of man's highest spiritual potential.

So the Christ's consciousness is found secretly written in the facade of Chartres.

Well, just let me say this. About the year 1200, which is almost precisely the date of the facade, an abbot, Joachim of Floris, wrote of three stages of the spirit after the Fall. The first stage is the age of the Father and the Jewish race—the covenant with the Hebrew people, preparing a priestly race which would be eligible to become the vehicle of the Incarnation. The second stage is the age of the Son, who is now to speak to the world through the institution of the Church. The third is the age of the Holy Ghost, in which the Spirit speaks directly to the individual. And this started a great vogue of hermit life in the thirteenth century. Saint Francis was thought to be the first representative of the stage of the Spirit.

I really believe that now we are finally getting it that way— the Spirit comes directly to people. And with that, according to Joachim of Floris, the institution of the Church would fall away.

Do you think the Dead Sea Scrolls and those found at Qumrān will change our understanding of Christianity?

I think the Dead Sea Scrolls belong to what I would call the old days: the Sons of Light against the Sons of Darkness. That's tied to the historical concept, and the symbols are read historically: *we* are the Sons of Light, and *they* are the Sons of Darkness, and we're going to be the glorious ones. Whereas in the Nag-Hammadi finds, those Coptic papers talk about the brotherhood of all—which is a Gnostic tradition. And there's that wonderful last answer in the Thomas Gospel when the disciples ask Jesus, "When will the kingdom come?" Now, the orthodox tradition has it that the kingdom will come historically. But the answer given in the Gnostic Gospel is that the kingdom comes psychologically, and not by expectation.

This is a change in the point of view: it's a change of perspective. You can look on the other person as an "It," or you can look on the other person as your brother or sister, and consequently the whole world changes.

So, do you think that these texts will come into Christianity?

Well, the first reactions have been negative. The pulpit doesn't want this message; the Church wants it that "We have It."

There was a fascinating moment in New York City when the Dalai Lama arrived, and the first welcome was at St. Patrick's Cathedral. There they were, the Catholic clergy, the Eastern Orthodox clergy, the rabbis, Protestant ministers, and so forth; and the whole sense of Buddhism is that all traditions intend the same end, and are ways to it. And the Dalai Lama, seeing these people there, made this point. Well, Cardinal Cooke had to let his members of the group know that that is not so: only the Catholics, we, have It. There they were, sitting around the table—rabbis, Protestant ministers, Catholic priests—putting on this show of accord, but each one holding his cards close and thinking he had the trump. But the only way you can go is by yielding the trump.

Well, two or three days later, there was a meeting of the Buddhist communities in New York, at the Cathedral of St. John the Divine. Over a thousand people attended, and it was conducted as though we were in the Jokang Temple in Lhasa, with chants and the distribution of *prasad* and buttered tea— thank God it wasn't yak butter, otherwise it would have been rancid. And then the Dalai Lama spoke. He said, "Keep up your practice. The results do not happen fast; this is no instant realization. And as you practice, you will become aware of a change of consciousness. Do not become attached to your method, for when your consciousness changes, you will recognize that all the methods are intending the one goal." That's the song mythology sings. It comes from the spirit of the human consciousness which becomes differently inflected from Germany to Japan to France to Iceland, or from the twelfth century to the twentieth. But those inflections are secondary.

What do you think will be the result of the influx of Eastern religions into Western culture?

You must remember that when we have teachers coming from the East, we're getting the best. There are also crude folk-traditions in the East; and we have the crude folk- traditions in the West; and our best teachers are not the ones that are most listened to. Let's put it that way, to start. Now, the best teaching from the East is the one given by the Dalai Lama. We also had it from Sri Ramakrishna, the great Indian Hindu teacher of the last century, namely that there is a common consciousness which is our own ground and so in conscious-ness we are one; insofar as you identify yourself with the consciousness that moves and lives in your body, you've iden-tified with that which you share with me. And on the other hand, if you fix on yourself, and your tradition, and believe you've got It, then you've removed yourself from the rest of mankind.

What the Eastern teachers are telling us is that the impor-tant thing is not what happened thousands of years ago when the Buddha was born or when Jesus was crucified: what's important is what's happening in you now. And what's impor-tant is not your membership in a religious community: it's what that membership is doing to your psyche. The divine lives within you. Our Western religions tend to put the divine outside of the earthly world and in God, in heaven. But the whole sense of the Oriental is that the kingdom of heaven is within you. Who's in heaven? God is. Where's God? God's within you. And what is God? God is a personification of that world-creative energy and mystery which is beyond thinking and beyond naming. We think not only that our God has been named and known, but that he's given us a whole system of rules. But this system of rules is not from God, it's from man, and the rules are man's clues as to how to get to the realization of God. Their view is quite different from that. When you hear it, you say, "Ah, yes."

Now the Waste Land might be said to be the taking of these rules literally, concretely; and the rejuvenation of the Arthurian grail hero, that of recognizing God as the dynamic of your own interior. Because we're all from a mysterious trans-rational ground—subatomic particles tell us that. We don't know what they are, and that's what we are. And of course our mind is in this world of time-space relationships; and the mind must open to the impulse and statements of this primary precedent of the general consciousness.

So we have effectively cut ourselves off from the spiritual side of life. Is that what you're saying? Or should I say that we restrict our spiritual inclinations to Sunday?

Well, during the industrial transformation of the world, the conditions of life lasted a little while; for generations they were essentially the same, so that the manner of dealing with them and getting the spiritual sense could be developed and richly experienced. But now the conditions of life change so rapidly that by the time you get yourself related to one set, another comes along. I think part of the anxiety of our time is the result of the rapidity with which change occurs; one cannot get a spiritual relationship to this rapidly changing practical problem.

Another important point that the Oriental traditions bring to us is that practical life is not separate from religious exercises. Religion isn't for Sunday or for Friday night; it is for all day every day. For instance, we're in a religious exercise right now, you and I, in our relationship. What is it that is playing in? It's through *life* that one is to experience the spirit and communicate the spirit and live in the spirit.

There's a wonderful little story about Sri Ramakrishna. A woman came to him and said,

"Master, I've had to admit to myself that I don't love God. I've tried to, but that's not where my love is."

"Well," he said, "Is there nothing in the world that you love?"

"Yes, I love my little nephew."

And he said, "There he is. In your service to this child, you are in service to the spirit that lives in that child which is the divine."

That's beautiful. And the same thing can be found in Zen Buddhism when someone asks the master,

"What is the Buddha?"

And he replies, "Have you had your breakfast?"

"Yes."

"Did you wash the dishes?"

"Yes."

"All right."

Another lesson in Buddhism is if you see the Buddha coming down the road, run away. Because if you concretize the divine in any fixed image and say "There it is" you're off course.

We're really talking about the Great Mystery, the ineffable.

That's what we're talking about. It's exciting to talk about it.

You mentioned the Waste Land. Could we say that in certain parts of American society a wasteland does exist?

I don't know what your impression is, Michael, but mine is that the majority of my friends are living Waste Land lives. In teaching, you have people who haven't come into the Waste Land yet. They're at the point of making the decision whether they're going to follow the way of their own zeal—the star that's dawned for them—or do what daddy and mother and friends want them to do. The adventure is always in the dark forest, and there's something perilous about it. Now, since retiring I've been lecturing for the most part to adults, many of whom feel they need a new start; they have to find a center in what they do that really meets their lives. And my impression is that many of my friends just are baffled; they're wandering in the Waste Land without any sense of where the water is—the source that makes things green.

You have to go beyond traditional concepts, don't you?

Indeed you do. Not only for your own life, but because life is different from the way it was and the rules of the past are restrictive of the life process. The moment the life process stops, it starts drying up; and the whole sense of myth is finding the courage to follow the process. In order to have something new, something old has to be broken; and if you're too heavily fixed on the old, you're going to get stuck. That's what hell is: the place of people who could not yield their ego system to allow the grace of a transpersonal power to move them.

So it's like coming in touch with the deeper part of life and being willing to let go.

And if you understand the spiritual aspect of your religious tradition, it will encourage you to do that. But if you interpret it in terms of hard fact, it's going to hinder you.

There are still millions who interpret the Bible literally.

Well, literal interpretation of the Bible faces the problem of scientific and historical research. We know that there was no Garden of Eden; we know that there was no Universal Flood. So we have to ask, what is the spiritual meaning of the Garden of Eden? What is the spiritual meaning of the Flood? Interpreting Biblical texts literally reduces their value; it turns them into newspaper reports. So there was a flood thousands of years ago. So what? But if you can understand what the Flood means in terms of a reference to spiritual circumstances—the coming of chaos, the loss of balance, the end of an age, the end of a psychological posture—then it begins to talk to you again.

I don't think many people know that other cultures have their own texts which refer to similar motifs.

Well, there's no doubt about it. The great German anthropologist, Adolf Bastian, was the first to note that, with very few exceptions, there are themes that occur in all the mythologies and all the religions of the world. He called these *elementary ideas*. Where do they come from? They don't come from the fact-world; they come from the psyche, just as fairy tales do. Then he also observed that, in the different provinces of mankind, they occur in different inflections, according to place and time. These he called *ethnic* or *folk ideas*.

These are the two sides to our subject. The folk idea is a historical problem: why do we have this form here and that one over there? But the elementary idea is a very deep psychological one. In India there are two words that refer to the two aspects of mythology: *desī*, which means local or provincial; and *marga*, meaning the path. And, by casting off the shell of the local, historical inflection, one comes to the elementary idea which is the path to one's own innermost heart. The word *marga* comes from the root word meaning the trail or path of an animal. So you follow the animal of the spiritual guide to your own inwardness. That's what myths are good for. And all the great traditions are talking to the same point.

It was through the ritual that societies expressed their feelings, and we don't have many rituals anymore.

It's astonishing how little ritual we have in our life—even the rituals of courtesy have gone. But the function of a ritual—a mythologically grounded ritual—is to engage you in the experience of the myth. A ritual is the enactment of a myth—either in a very literal way, or in an extremely abstract way. The ritual of the sacrifice of the Mass in the Roman Catholic Church is the re-enactment of the Crucifixion. So you're participating in the sense of the Crucifixion. And that sense of the Crucifixion is twofold. One is that the divine transcendent has come into the world and has accepted the crucifixion of life; the other is that the individual has yielded his individual self to the grace of a transpersonal realization. The Cross is the threshold of the passage of eternity into time and of time into eternity; and in participating in this, you are giving yourself to the Christ—and the Christ in you, namely the knower of the Father.

And so, understanding the Crucifixion in terms of its mythological or spiritual sense opens the image. Then it doesn't matter whether Christ lived or not. Actually there's no doubt that Jesus lived, that he was crucified, that he died and was buried. But it is a little more questionable as to whether he rose again and ascended to heaven. That doesn't matter; that's the mythological implication of giving yourself; he who loses his life shall find it. And this is what we call the creative act—not hanging on, but yielding to the new creative moment.

The Mass is a good example of the loss of meaningful ritual. It was changed to accommodate the changing times and, in doing so, we lost the original sense of the ritual.

Well, in my view, the Mass was a more potent ritual in Latin with the priest facing not the congregation, but the infinite transcendent. And as for the vernacular, well, the problem there is that one's vernacular language has all kinds of domestic and earthly and often just tawdry associations; whereas the other is sacred, and the pitch is heavenward. The wonderful power of ritualized language, the rhythms and so forth—you can never match a Gregorian chant in English with a Gregorian chant in the language it was meant to carry. So my view is that the Church has made a mistake. In fact, I think it's making a major mistake in not realizing that its function is to preserve a ritual and to let the individual experience that ritual in his own sense. Instead, the ritual is changed and the emphasis is on theological interpretation of the Eucharist and how to read it, so that you get all involved in rational matters, instead of the impact of losing yourself in the event.

Because Jesus' message was that each of us has the capacity to realize the highest potential.

Well, indeed! And that comes out strongly in the *Gospel According to Thomas,* in which Jesus says, "He who has heard and assimilated my word is as I." And that's good Buddhism! It's important to realize that it's right in you. And I think that's one of the things the Oriental teachers are telling us.

Now, of course, we get the quintessence of those Oriental teachings when they come over here. If you were to go to their country of origin, you'd find a lot of local *desī* or provincial material that would be just as much an encumbrance as the equivalent over here. So we're getting the real spiritual message; and what they're telling us is that these teachings have a spiritual, not a historical, concrete reference.

Heinrich Zimmer once said, "The best things can't be told; the second best are misunderstood; the third best have to do with history." Now, the vocabulary through which the best things are told as second best is the vocabulary of history, but it doesn't refer to history; it refers through this to the transcendent. Deities have to become, as one great German scholar said, "transparent to the transcendent." The transcendent must show and shine through those deities. But it must shine through us, too, and through the spiritual things we are talking about. And as long as you keep pinning it down to concrete fact, and declare something isn't true because it didn't happen, you're wrong. We don't say that about fairy tales, and so we get the truth of them. We should read our religions that way.

Is there a difference between cults and religion?

Christianity was a cult, certainly, in the Roman period before it became a dominant culture-structuring power. The cult is the beginning of a social structure, living like a parasite, as it were, on an already structured society. The intensity of the cult comes from the force of the psychological need to establish relationships that seem significant in a world where the relationships are not significant. Do you see what I mean?

Yes.

And so the people are pulled in a very, very deep way. It's almost like the passion of love or lust. It's deeply grounded, and people's minds are out of control. It's a natural thing to happen to people who have been utterly deprived of mythologically informed relationships. When you look at the history of the European city, you quickly realize that the focal point is the cathedral or church. On your approach to Chartres even today, the first thing you see is the cathedral. In the princely periods of the seventeenth and eighteenth centuries, the most important building was the palace—there's a shift of accent from the religious to the social-political.

When you approach a great city today, what you see are commercial buildings and dwellings. The palace is diminished and the church even more so.

Salt Lake City is a microcosm of that phenomena. Salt Lake City was founded as a religious community and in the center— the perfect old Chaldean way of doing it—is the temple from which, in the four directions, spread the main streets. Now, there's another building that was built later as the political center—a kind of capitol building, and it's higher than the temple. That was the second stage. But *the* big building there now houses the bureaucracy of the Mormon Church. But just think of living a life that is governed by political-economic concerns, with no sense of where the cathedral or temple should be. It's out of center, you might say; and this is the way our psyches are. But the temple is important: the sense of the mystery, the gratitude for being alive, the sense of transcendent energy that unites all of us, coordinates our cities, coordinates our lives. That's all been lost; and having lost that, people search with terrific voracity after any clue that will help them find it again. And that's what the cult is.

But the cult does not work as a total city-structuring force. There's another structure principle there, and so people lose their minds, lose their centers. It's a very easy thing to understand.

In the Hellenistic period, all kinds of cults abounded. Christianity was but one of them, and it finally won through.

I would add that these little groups—these cults today—represent attempts to break out of an archaic institution. Our religious institutions are archaic—that is clear. And the individual finds himself not at ease within them.

The cults are usually oversimplifications: life could be much simpler, and all of that. Many of them think of going away to far places and setting up a whole new community. This was the case all through the nineteenth century in America. Mormonism is one example that comes to mind. The individual is not able to do anything alone; life consists in a relationship. And even though one is living an individual life—not following the formulae of the past—one has to have some kind of companionship and response. The cult seems to offer that echo to people, and many of those people in cults are not greatly individual; they don't have the courage of their own individuality; they follow the lead of someone who seems to be an individual. That is respect for the individual, you might say, but it's too bad that a possibility of fulfillment doesn't come out of these things. They are all in-group things again: "We're special, we've got The Message and the world is evil." The answer isn't there.

What about the desire to follow a guru? We see religions and cults based on the teacher-disciple relationship flourishing everywhere.

I think that is bad news. I really do think you can take clues from teachers—I know you can. But, you see, the traditional

Oriental idea is that the student should submit absolutely to the teacher. The guru actually assumes responsibility for the student's moral life, and this is total giving. I don't think that's quite proper for a Western person. One of the big spiritual truths for the West is that each of us is a unique creature, and consequently has a unique path.

There's one quotation I ran into in *La Queste del Saint Graal* which hit me as being the essence of what I'd call the European or Western spirituality. The knights of King Arthur's court were seated at table and Arthur would not let the meal be served until an adventure had occurred. And, indeed, an adventure did occur. The Grail itself appeared, carried by angelic miracle, covered, however, by a cloth. Everyone was in rapture and then it withdrew. Arthur's nephew Gawain stood up and said, "I propose a vow. I propose that we should all go in pursuit of this Grail to behold it unveiled." And it was determined that that was what they would do. And then occur these lines which seem to me so wonderful: "They thought it would be a disgrace to go forth in a group. Each entered the forest that *he* had chosen where there was no path and where it was darkest." Now, if there's a way or path, it's someone else's way; and the guru has a path for you. He knows where you are on it. He knows where he is on it, namely, way ahead. And all you can do is get to be as great as he is. This is a continuation of the dependency of childhood; maturity consists in outgrowing that and becoming your own authority for your life. And this quest for the unknown seems so romantic to Oriental people. What is unknown is the fulfillment of your own unique life, the likes of which has never existed on the earth. And you are the only one who can do it. People can give you clues how to fall down and how to stand up; but when to fall and when to stand, and when you are falling, and when you are standing, this only you can know. And in the way of your own talents is the only way to do it.

If you go out for athletics, the coach doesn't tell you exactly how to hold your arms; he watches you run, estimates your form, and tunes you up a little bit. It's *your* way and that's the way of the whole life, it seems to me. This is why I don't think the guru thing is as great as it's supposed to be. It's an Oriental idea where the uniqueness of the individual is utterly disregarded. I think I'm right there. I've spent a long time with Oriental studies, and I see *nothing* that does not say each has the law of his caste or his tradition or his church to follow.

Yeats, in *A Vision*, speaks of the two masks that life wears. The first is the primary mask that the society has put upon you—the technique of life. But in adolescence the individual has a sense of a potentiality within himself that has to throw off that mask and find what Yeats calls "the antithetical mask"—the mask contrary to that of society. And then comes that struggle so characteristic of youth in our society. In the traditional society, you are not allowed to follow the antithetical; the primary is there like a cookie-mold on you. But here comes this struggle. Now, if the family or society opposes that, it becomes rather fierce. But with a gradual yielding and attention, the young person can learn his own possibilities and what they can do for him. This is the proper way.

Furthermore, there's something else about the guru: it's becoming more and more a concern to me with my friends and former students. When you start an inward meditation under a guru, the problem is the relationship of your ego to the self. That's the primary relationship—consciousness to a deeper self. And other relationships—relationships to your wife, to your friends—become intrusions. Do you see what I mean? Whereas, taking the other way, let's say of marriage, that is an exercise in amplification of ego, opening of ego—the grace of participation in another life. That's a religious exercise. That's why marriage is a sacrament. That's why the two make one. Well, if that's the main relationship problem in your life, then how are you going to handle this other one at the same time? Furthermore, most gurus are not married and they don't know anything about that.

We've been talking about the Eastern guru, but we also have gurus in the West. I think of people in the human potential movement, for example: there are people who have taken on the role of guru.

They themselves are following an Oriental model, I would say. But it must be *really* flattering to say, "Are you enlightened? I am! So listen! I don't take any guff." One of the typical things in the Orient is that any criticism disqualifies you for the guru's instruction. Well, in heaven's name, is that appropriate for a Western mind? It's simply a transferring of your submission to the childhood father onto a father for your adulthood, which means you're not growing up.

Similarly in psychoanalysis there's the whole idea of transference. What do you transfer to the analyst? You transfer all the parental systems of relationships, so you're still bound; you're still a submissive and dependent person.

When you talk about maturity in adulthood, I think of what Jesus said, "You must become as a little child to enter the kingdom of heaven." Let's juxtapose that with adulthood and maturity. How do those two come together?

I think what he was talking about is spontaneity. But the answer to your question comes from Nietzsche in the introduction to *Zarathustra*. It's curious to speak of Nietzsche in the same breath as Jesus because typically he's thought to be the anti-Christ; he even thought so himself a little bit. But these are two great teachers, and great teachers frequently say similar things in different languages. Nietzsche says there are three stages to the spirit. The first is that of the camel. The camel gets down on his knees and says, "Put a load on me." This is the condition of youth and learning. When the camel is well loaded, he gets to his feet and runs out into the desert. This is the place where he's going to be alone to find himself and he's transformed into a lion. And the function and deed of the lion is to kill a dragon, and that dragon's name is "Thou shalt." On every scale of the dragon, a law is written, some dating from 2000 B.C., others from yesterday's paper. When the camel is well loaded, the lion is potent and the dragon *is* killed. You see, there are two quite different things. One is submission, obedience, learning; the other is strong and assertive. And when the dragon is killed, the lion is transformed into a child. In Nietzsche's words, "a wheel rolling out of its own center." That's what the child represents in this mystical language. The human being has recovered that spontaneity and innocence and thought-lessness of rules which is so marvelous in childhood. The little one who comes up and says absolutely embarrassing things to the stranger who's visiting your house— that's the child: not the obedient child, but the innocent child who is spontaneous and has the courage to live its impulses.

How might we as individuals get in touch with the child that lies within us?

By killing the dragon, "Thou shalt."

By choosing not to live by other people's rules?

Right. Respecting them, but not living by them. Respecting them more or less in the way you respect the red and green lights on the highway. There are other rules which seem advisable—if, in your own intelligence, you see that such a rule represents human decency, for example. But a rule put on you as a rule—"Thou shalt not"—is another show. I think one can learn to take courage; it also involves taking responsibility for what you're doing—taking the rap, if you have made radical mistakes and hurt people. It can be done.

I've come across references to the Hermetic Circle lately. Precisely what does that refer to?

What we call the Hermetic tradition really dates from the late Hellenistic period, first centuries B.C. and A.D. And as I understand it, what took place during that time was an amalgamation which is very much like our own, in that culture forms of quite different origin came crashing together and influenced each other. There was the Greek world with Hermes, the guide to immortal life; and there was Thoth, who is the mythological counterpart in the Egyptian world. And these two were brought together, particularly in the time of the Ptolemies in Egypt. The combination of these two created a new legendary figure called Hermes Trismegistus [Hermes Thrice-Blessed] who was thought to have been a historical character. So, you have a legend about this assumed historical character who is supposed to have been a contemporary of Moses. There was a question as to whether Moses learned from him or he from Moses, or whether both of them learned from the goddess Isis.

Now, the distinction between the Mosaic doctrine and the Hermetic doctrine is that the symbols which are shared are interpreted historically by the Mosaic tradition, and in the Hermetic tradition they are interpreted spiritually. So there grew, during those first centuries of Christianity, a whole literature of the Hermetic sort in which the symbols, interpreted in the orthodox Christian tradition as historical, were being read in a proper mythological sense. And these then began to link the Christian myth to pagan analogues. The Gnostics, for instance, were in that boat. But the orthodox Christians insisted on the historicity of all these events. And then, in the fourth and fifth centuries, when the canon of the New Testament was put together, all those stories which were obviously symbolic were eliminated and what were conceived to be historical documents were retained. But even those, of course, were mythological. The virgin birth, death and resurrection, ascension to heaven, and all those kinds of things were taken to be literal facts. And so, today when, for instance, the ascension into heaven is translated into physics, it becomes ridiculous because there's no place to go; and the body, even going with the speed of light, wouldn't be out of the galaxy yet.

So the physical interpretation is lost and the symbol itself is lost, because it has been interpreted that way.

You see, these symbols are the vehicles of communication between conscious and unconscious systems. And when this connection is broken, people feel rootless. But it's all right here; all you have to do is turn in.

The Trinity is another symbol that we see all over, isn't it?

Well, it comes in various forms and with various interpretations. The number three can be read in many ways, but the traditional Western interpretation is Father, Son, and Holy Ghost. The Father is symbolic of, or the personification of, the ultimate divine. For the Father to be known, there must be a knower. God can be known only by God, therefore the second Person of the Blessed Trinity is the Knower—the Son. And when there is a knower and the known, there is a relationship between the two, and this is Holy Spirit. Now, this can be translated into Sanskrit as *sat-chit-ananda. Sat* means being— that's the Father; *chit* is consciousness—this is the Son knowing the Father; *ananda* is rapture or bliss—that's the relationship of the Father to the Son. There's a precise counterpart there. This is a fascinating realization.

Death and eternity play a large part in our thinking. Does that interfere with our perception of death?

Eternity is not a continuation of time. Eternity is a dimension of here and now. And we have eternal life now. This is what is meant by "The kingdom of the Father is spread over the earth and men do not see it." When one thinks of what happens after death, one is still thinking in temporal terms. So, when we're talking about symbolic systems, that is a misplaced concern. Do you see? You've got to do something else with it; you've got to spiritualize the symbol.

My favorite definition of religion is "a misinterpretation of mythology." And the misinterpretation consists precisely in attributing historical references to symbols which properly are spiritual in their reference. What a mythic image talks about is not something that happened somewhere or will happen somewhere at some time or other; it refers to what is now, and was yesterday, and will be tomorrow, and is forever.

So the Apocalypse is something that's with us all the time.

The moment you see this kingdom of the Father spread over the earth, the Apocalypse has occurred. It's a perpetual potential, and it's also something in a person who has the experience, that shuts on and off.

There's a wonderful Indian story of a young man who was told by his guru, "You are Brahman. You are God." What a thing to experience! "I am God." So, deeply indrawn, this young man goes out for a walk. He walks through the village, goes out into the country. And coming down the road is a great elephant, with the howdah on top, and the driver on his head. And the young man, thinking "I am God. I am God," does not get out of the way of the elephant. The mahout shouts, "Get out of the way, you lunatic!" The young man hears him and looks and sees the elephant, and he says to himself, "I am God and the elephant is God. Should God get out of the way of God?" And of course the moment of truth arrives when the elephant suddenly wraps his trunk around him and tosses him off the road.

The young man goes back to his guru in a disheveled condition—not physically hurt, but psychologically in shock. The guru sees him and asks, "Well, what happened to you?"

The young man tells him his story and then says, "You told me that I was God."

"And so you are."

"The elephant is God."

"And so it is."

"Well, then, should God get out of the way of God?"

"But why didn't you listen to the voice of God shouting from the head of the elephant?"

There are two perspectives, and what happens with the

neophyte mystic is that he doesn't know how to live on the two planes.

We certainly have a lot of neophyte mystics, I think.

The world's bubbling with them, right now. They're very charming, but they're in trouble often.

The alchemist of the thirteenth century was a kind of mystic, wasn't he?

Yes, you could say that. The main theme in alchemy is the transmutation of matter: transmuting base matter into gold. And, in the texts that have come to us from the sixteenth and seventeenth centuries, the alchemists make a point that the gold they're interested in is not the gold of commerce; it is the gold of spiritual fulfillment and realization. And the image of the base matter out of which the gold is to come is comparable, by analogy, to the Christian image of the Old Adam and the New Adam; so that the main idea in alchemy is really one of psychological or spiritual transformation, fulfillment, and illumination. There certainly were alchemists who were trying to get physical gold. But always when you read the texts, it becomes apparent that the transformations in the retort are associated with visionary images.

painter

The thing I like to compare it to, in my own attempt to understand it all, is painting. The artist has a frame that is noncommittal—it's a kind of void—and he projects something of his own imaginative creation into that by way of paints. It's important to him whether this color is here and that color over there is in exactly that place. And it isn't always just reproducing as a camera might; it's something of his own spirit that's put forth, and it bounces back to him, telling something about his inner spirit.

Well, the alchemist used metals and various chemical substances in a way the painter uses paint; and his retort—the Hermetic retort, sealed by Hermes, the god who gives us the knowledge of immortal life—is, as it were, the canvas. By dropping certain substances into the retort and watching them send up mists and so on, he activated his own imagination. And through that, he brought up, into the field of his consciousness, potentialities from his more unconscious system.

This process wasn't practiced for 500 or so years simply to get gold which never appeared. There were deeper realizations which were intended, realizations of bringing forth the gold from primal matter—the matter of transformation now—bringing forth the gold of the new human being from the primal matter of our different local civilizations. There is an analogy there.

It is, by analogy, associated with the salvation of man through the birth of the Christ from the womb of an earthly being. That's the comparable image. Mythology is basically a system of analogies: as gold from base matter, so immortal life from mortal life; so the Christ from Adam. The symbols tell you something about the bringing forth of the gold of your own spirit.

Organized religion has always taken a dim view of alchemy. Is that because of the kind of transformation you're talking about?

There's a slightly different theory underlying alchemy about the world: the gold is in the substance of the world; a savior doesn't have to bring it in from without. It's a world-operation. Many of the institutional religions are more interested in the institution than in the transformation of life, and anything that can effect the transformation outside of the servants of the institution is an anathema.

There were many alchemists in the Middle Ages who were persecuted by the Church.

Yes. But there were many who were very important philosophers. Albertus Magnus, the master of Thomas Aquinas, was interested in alchemy. And a work called *Aurora Consurgens* is attributed to Aquinas, although it may not actually be his work. But the attribution would not have been made had Aquinas himself not been interested in alchemy.

I want to get back to the interpretation of myth, and especially relative to Christianity. What is your experience with people from the established religions? How do you convey to them that it is possible to look at the Bible from a symbolic point of view?

I taught a course at Sarah Lawrence College on comparative mythology for thirty-eight years. I taught young people of every available creed. More than fifty percent of my students from the New York area were Jewish; many were Christians— Protestant, Catholic; there were Mormons and Zoroastrians and Buddhists. There wasn't much of a problem with the Buddhists, but all the others were somewhat stuck in their provincial traditions.

It was the simplest thing; all I did was to point out the parallels and identities all over the place. You see, when there is a motif—such as that of the virgin birth—which occurs in American Indian mythologies, in Greek mythology, and so on, it becomes obvious that the virgin birth could not have referred to a historical event. It's a spiritual event that's referred to—even in the Christian tradition. One after another, these motifs became spiritualized instead of historicized. And the interesting thing is that instead of the person losing her religion, she gained it. It became a religion instead of a misleading theory.

How can a theologian in a seminary present a course in comparative religion and still hold fast to literal interpretations?

This is the most baffling mystery of my experience. Because I know, from associating with my colleagues, that a great many of these gentlemen become firm. "Ours is finally different. It's a fact!"

You mentioned the Flood. Like the Virgin Birth, it also is a motif that runs through all cultures.

Yes. There are very few cultures that don't have a Flood motif. That's a basic idea: the dissolution of the world which takes place every night when we go into the flood of our own unconscious. It's the analogue of the mythological Flood: at the end of the cycle, there's a flood. The American Indians have lots of Flood stories.

It was thought when the diggings in the Tigris-Euphrates Valley were proceeding that evidence of the Biblical flood could be located—at least a flood universal to that area. And there were flood levels found in several cities. But they were not the same flood level; they were local floods. There's no cosmic flood; the Flood motif is a mythological idea. The whole notion that all originates from water, and all is going back to water, gives you a cycle: out of water, back to water, out of water, back to water; and each new cosmic aeon, each new world-age, is, as it were, a creation out of water and a dissolution into water. So it's a mythological motif. This is exactly the point that Thomas Mann makes very well in the first part of *Joseph and His Brothers*: the archetypal Flood is a mythological, a psychological flood, and when local floods occur they become identified with it. Do you understand? We have experienced The Flood. The Flood is a mythological principle, and when a flood occurred, we understood the sense of the image.

And this motif is universal?

Mythological floods are found among practically every people of the world. All along the equatorial belt, up in the North, on the American plains. There's a rather amusing variation by the Blackfoot Indians. The flood has come, and on a raft is an old man or trickster hero with a bunch of little animals. In order to re-create the world, he sends them down to bring up mud. Two or three of the animals die on the way, and finally the muskrat comes up with a little bit of mud. The old man puts the mud on the water, pronounces magical words, and the world is brought into being.

In Siberia, and in areas close to old Eastern Orthodox Russia, there is the same story. But the man on the raft is Christ, and the diver is the Devil. Christ sends the Devil down to get the mud and when he takes it out of the Devil's mouth, the Devil holds some of it back. And as Christ makes a nice smooth earth, the Devil spits the mud out and that becomes the mountains.

So, there is a Flood myth that runs all the way from Western Asia to the American plains, and quite a different flood story from the ones found in Australia, or the Tasmanian Islands, or pygmy Africa.

What does contemporary religion have to do with the adventure?

I think contemporary religion is in a very bad spot. And I think it is because it has taken the symbols as the referents. Religion is the constellation of metaphors, and the metaphor points to connotations that are of the spirit, not of history, as I said before. And in our religions, we're accenting the historical image that carries the message, but we stay with the image.

The literal interpretation, in other words . . .

Yes, and you lose these messages. The thing about Jesus is not that he died and was resurrected, but that his death and resurrection must tell us something about our own spirit.

Why do you think we tend to a literal interpretation of Christ in myth?

I think it's the result of a strong institutional emphasis in our religions in the West, and a fear of the mystical experience. In fact, the experience of the divine within you is regarded as *blasphemy.* I remember having given a lecture once on this problem of becoming transparent to transcendence, so that your life becomes a transparency through which light shines. I spoke of it as "the god in you, coming *out* through your life." A couple of months later, I met a young woman at another talk who had happened to be present at the first one; and she told me that when I had said "The Christ in you asks you to live," a priest sitting next to her had said, "That's blasphemy!" So, in institutional religion, all the spirit is out there somewhere, not in you.

But what's the meaning of the saying, "The kingdom of heaven is within you," if you can't say, "It's within me"? Then who's in heaven?

And, "I and the Father are one."

All of that. Jesus was crucified because he said, "I and the Father are one." Well, the ultimate mystical experience is of one's identity with the divine power. That's the sense of the *Chandogya Upanishad* saying which says "You are It." That divinity which you seek outside, and which you first become aware of because you recognize it outside, is actually your inmost being. Now, it's not a nice thing to say, but it's not good for institutions if people find that it's all within themselves. So there may be some point there about our particular situation in the West where religious institutions have been able to dominate a society.

It's interesting how they handle this in India. The first half of your life is spent in the society, obeying the rules, following the rules of your caste and worshiping the local images of the divine power. But then there comes the time when you should go into the forest. You give up your caste and everything else, and so the life is divided in half: first the life in the society, and then the life in the forest.

The problem, I think, for Western man is to have the two together, so that you're living the life *in* the society all *through* your life—no quitting in mid-life and going off and having the high realization, but through the actual living of your life, to realize the play of the divine mystery, not only in yourself, but through your friends *and* your enemies.

And I think that that's the only possible meaning of Jesus' saying, "Love your enemies." He didn't say don't have enemies, but have the compassion of recognizing the divine power in *them* as well as in you. And in the field of time there are always pairs of opposites. It's got to be that way! It can't be otherwise. And to realize that's the way the One plays through the many is the trick. Do you understand what I'm saying?

Yes. But in contemporary society, we hear about the separation of Church and State, and at the same time, we have a situation in which morality and religion and politics are being wrapped up into one thing.

It's too tight a bundle. Ethics and religion are not the same. Religion has a mystical dimension, and that's what it's really all about. Ethics has to do with social values and religion has to do with personal, inward realization. Those are different things! And living in a society defines your realization of the inward values through the ethics of society. That's the trick, I might say, of being alive in the world.

When we look at contemporary life, however, and then look at our institutions, it's very rarely that we deal with principles such as integrity, ethics, or life of the spirit. If we looked at every bill that comes up before Congress and gets passed, in terms of its ethical nature or its ethical consequences, what a different light that would cast on the passage of laws!

I think one of the problems of modern life is the rapidity with which social values change, and they change inevitably, because life-conditions change. So there's a lag, and one doesn't know how to evaluate certain things in terms of the contemporary conditions. But politics has to deal with the contemporary moment. And so, there you are: you're up against a blank wall. It's almost like the creative world that we were talking about. It's the adventure. We are in a free fall into Future. Society itself is on the adventure, and so it's awfully hard to evaluate situations.

What has happened in this country over the past thirty or forty years, with immigration of people from totally unforeseen places, people with life values totally different from those of the people who instituted this country? We can no longer hold on with confidence to the system which once worked—the country has got to open now to other things. For instance, I'm living in Hawaii. I think the majority of the people living in Hawaii are not Christians. There are a lot of Japanese, a lot of Chinese . . . well, Filipinos frequently are Catholic. But the saying "In God we trust" doesn't mean a damn thing to a Buddhist.

I had a very amusing experience shortly after arriving in Honolulu. I was invited to give a talk in a church which happened to be the one with which my wife's family was associated. When I married Jean, we went to that church and, having been brought up a Roman Catholic, I had never seen a Protestant service. To me, it seemed just a kind of meeting: there was no blessed sacrament; there was no God in the house, and so forth.

Well, some time later, they had lectures on Buddhism and were told that the Buddhists don't believe in God. So they wondered how Buddhists could have a spiritual life, not believing in God.

I took my cue from that, and pointed out that when I came to Hawaii and experienced my first Protestant service, I was surprised to find that they didn't have God in the tabernacle. So, the Protestants don't have God in the tabernacle, and the Buddhists don't have God in their vocabulary.

The God image is a metaphor for a spiritual experience. But you don't have to get it through that particular metaphor. This was something that I thought was an amusing teaser. Well . . .

In some sense, we create our own gods.

Yes, that's exactly what we do. No matter what name we give it, the God we have is the one we're capable of having. That's something people don't realize. Simply because they're all saying the same name for God, that doesn't mean they have the same relationship to That, or the same concept of what It is. And the concept of God is only a foreground of the experience. Well, there you are . . . As Meister Eckhart wrote—

—*A number of Zen roshis have called him very Buddhist.*

—Yes. As he said in his sermon "On Riddance," the ultimate riddance, and the most difficult, is the getting rid of your god to go to God. Wow! That's the big adventure, isn't it? That's the ultimate adventure. That's what you have to strive for every minute of your life: to get rid of the life that you have planned in order to have the life that's waiting to be yours. Move. Move. Move into the Transcendent. That's the whole sense of the adventure, I think.

There is talk of a synthesis of East and West, taking the best from both cultures. What do you think of the future of that?

I don't think there can be a general synthesis of East and West. But there can be special syntheses in different places. I think what the West absorbs from the East is going to be one thing; what the East absorbs from the West is going to be quite something else. And it will differ from region to region. The Chinese are not going to want the same things the Indians are going to want—not only want, but need in the way of spiritual food. The West has spiritual food to give, not just gadgets.

Now, I can't talk about what's happening in India, because I'm not an Indian and I look at it as an outsider. Likewise with Japan, although I admire enormously what the Japanese are doing with our Western things; but they're still Japanese. But I can say something about the East coming to the West, particularly in the field of religion and mythology.

Our Western systems have been institutionalized from way

back, but particularly from the fourth century in the period of Theodosius. Our mythologies are institutionalized and salvation comes from membership in an institution. You see the signs all over New York subways: "Go to Church," "Read the Bible." That has to do with one definition of a religious life. You can't find it in yourself; you find it only through the Church. These men from the East come—whether they're Indians or Japanese or Tibetans—and they tell you that the real mystery is in yourself. We have that in our mystic tradition also—not what the Church advertises. Finding the divine not only within you, but within all things, is not favored by either the Jewish or the Christian or the Muslim religion. And what the Orient brings is a realization of the inward way. When you sit in meditation with your hands in your lap, with your head looking down, that means you've gone in and you're coming not just to a soul that is disengaged from God: you're coming to that divine mystery right there in yourself.

So there's the mythical attraction. At the same time we do see people essentially changing their lifestyle—and their clothing—when following gurus.

There are two responses that are quite natural to the guru. When anyone becomes a model for you, you tend automatically to imitate him. This is the spontaneous identification, and it's through such identification that something inside develops in you. The second phase is finding your own self. I think that wearing Oriental clothes or assuming Oriental names is not the correct way to go about it. You've displaced again; you have mistaken the clothing for the message, and not everyone who says, "Lord, Lord," is going to get to the kingdom of heaven; not everyone who wears a turban is a released spirit. That's one way to get caught again. Then you mistake a certain attitude or manner of living that has nothing to do with the spiritual life.

I've heard of a couple of roshis over here whose first statement was: "If you want illumination, you've got to be an American, not a Japanese." To make believe that you're Japanese is just to run off on a detour and get stuck in the woods. It's not in the manner of dress or speech; it's the manner of experience and illumination. So I think the guru can be a delusion. But *everything* can be deluding. The thing about the guru in the West is that he represents an alien principle of the spirit, namely, that you don't follow your own path; you follow a given path. And that's totally contrary to the Western spirit! Our spirituality is of the individual quest, individual realization—authenticity in your life out of your own center. So you must take the message from the East, assimilate it to your own dimension and to your own thrust of life, and not get pulled off track.

As I said, the great message of the Oriental teachers is already in our mystic tradition. For instance, there's a wonderful little mystic named Angelus Silesius (1624–1677)—I always think of him as a little man because he rendered his message in very short, two-line verses, one of which runs:

"Of what use Gabriel, your message to Marie,
Unless you can now give the same message to me!"

In other words, the Christ should be born in him. And if it's not born in you, well then, the religion hasn't worked. And whether you call it the Christ, or the Buddha, or cosmic consciousness, or whatever, it's the one message that these different religions are delivering; and unless you read them in terms of an inner life, you have lost your own ground and base.

So Jesus as a teacher of experience has been lost in Christian culture, which leaves us with the College of Cardinals telling us what to do.

Exactly. You can see this in the *Gospel According to Thomas*, when Jesus says, "He who drinks of my mouth will be become as I am, and I am he." Now, that's Gnosticism, that's Buddhism. We're all Buddha-beings; we're all Christ-beings. And the difference between you and me and the Buddha is that he knew how to live in terms of Buddha-consciousness instead of his own individual interests; and living in Christ is comparable, using the Christian terminology. It's fascinating to compare the language of Christian and Buddhist teachings. And it's in this comparative way that you can learn from another tradition—you see an aspect of your own. And it's particularly important for us since our tradition has been institutionally dominated—we need the Orient to teach us about the aspect of personal experience in religion.

There may even have been an actual interchange between the Buddhists and the early Christians.

I'm completely convinced that there was. All along the Silk Road from Aleppo to Ch'ang-an in China there were Nestorian, Christian, Manichaean, and Buddhist chapels and temples. Furthermore, the distances between the centers in the East and those in the West were not great and there was traffic back and forth along with delegations from India to Rome, and vice versa. Ashoka, the great Buddhist monarch of India, sent missionaries to Alexandria in the third century B.C. And when you realize that Alexandria was one of the centers from which Christianity took its theology, you realize that the relationship between Buddhism and Christianity was inevitable. Look at the doctrine of Christ from the standpoint of Buddhism, and the Christ is a Bodhisattva—the one who comes with love to participate in the sorrows of the world. But I think too much has been made of the suffering of Jesus.

There is another kind of crucifix which is called "Christ Triumphant"—he's there with eyes open. Augustine says Christ went to the cross as a bridegroom to his bride—there's that movement into life with zeal. All life is suffering, but the Buddha and Christ were concerned with fulfilling the spiritual dynamic.

This whole idea of following the life of the spirit, and having to give up—I think there's a lot of misunderstanding about what that surrender means. It's really, in mythological terms, a surrender to the god within, isn't it?

Yes. But, you know, the god within may not have very much respect for the life that you've got to lead, so you've got to keep God from pushing you too hard. Do you see what I mean? Let him come slowly, because being God is not being on earth. God himself had to descend and get crucified to be on earth. And that business of not getting quite crucified is the task.

Do you see other parallels in the Buddhist tradition with other cultures? Some of their deities are based on actual historical figures. I think of the Tibetan Buddhist pantheon of deities which each represent a particular aspect of life.

You see, in Tibet, as in certain other parts of the Orient, there was an enormous emphasis on meditation, and the inflections of experience that come through meditation; and each of these inflections had personifications. The reason there was the enormously complex pantheon was because of the tradition of inward experience. Whereas, if you don't go inward and have all these varieties of experience, then such deities don't mean anything to you. The Tibetan pantheon in its fullness would not mean anything to a Western person, because he hasn't had the counterpart experiences. But a monk who has spent his whole life meditating is in tune with that pantheon.

Now, regarding actual historical figures: they were teachers, and they have been glorified. The pantheon of Tibet, if you can call it that, is particularly interesting because it's interpreted and understood in psychological terms all the way. That's the great thing about the whole Buddhist tradition. The forms are not deified, however; they are not concretized in the absolute sense. What they represent are aspects of the psyche, and by contemplating them you are activating those energies in yourself.

There is a motif called a *yidam* or, in Sanskrit, *Ishtadevata*—that is, you have your chosen deity and what that deity represents is an imaging out before you of aspects of your own psyche which are going to operate for your illumination. The figure in itself has no concrete reality except as a carrier, a mirror of your own psychological potentials: you choose it and you let that be your model. And when you're dealing with your guru, who is your guide, he is experienced as that *yidam*. This is the way the Tibetan pantheon works.

So, every one of these figures, essential ones, is manifest in at least three aspects: its peaceful aspect, in which it is experienced without ego-fear; its operative aspect, in which it is operating on you and you're receiving it; and, finally, its horrific aspect, which you try to hold to yourself. The *yidam* will give all these aspects and other related powers which you are to realize as of your own nature. This is a wonderful thing. And since meditation is the major occupation in the monasteries, there's a great sophistication in identifying within oneself aspects of commitment and potentiality. But they're not like Yahweh: they are potentials of the psyche and operative forces in it.

I'm reminded of a chapter in Lama Govinda's book, The Way of the White Clouds, *in which he talks about how one of the lamas actually becomes one of these horrific deities during a ritual. His description of that transformation was a delight to read.*

That was possession. And since the power is within you, it can become dominant, and your features will be transformed. Possession takes place even in very simple fields like that of voodoo. In the rituals of the peristyle, in the little temple compound of a houngan or priest, people dance and invoke a deity; then somebody is taken and becomes that deity, which is recognized by the way the person behaves. If the deity is Guede, for example, who is the god of death [in the voodoo tradition of Haiti], the person can drink things that would burn your gut out. In fact, one of the tests that determines the presence of Guede in a person is to give him a concoction—it's got everything in it. And if the deity's present, the person can drink it; otherwise he can't.

Is this the same as Avatars?

This is a different show now. This isn't an Avatar in the sense of a deity coming down from above. Avatar means "down-coming." There's a different context of thought associated with bringing something out of the psyche from putting something *into* the psyche. For instance, the big question in Christianity was whether Mary gave birth to a Christ or just to Jesus in whom the Christ-principle descended at the time of the baptism, when the heavens opened and the voice of God said, "This is my beloved Son . . ." Historians believe that the possession took place at that moment.

That is the concept of two worlds: a world of spirit, and a world of mortal bodies into which the spirit descends. But I don't hold with that idea. I accept it as a mythological motif, and I'm interested in it as a scholar. But if I interpret possession, I'm going to do so in psychological terms—something from inside has assumed control of the body. Possession from outside, in the way of devil possession, I don't know what to say about that.

What about Hell; where does that idea come from in Christianity?

Saint Thomas Aquinas, I guess. I don't know who came up with that horrible thought! Christianity is the only religion with that concept. I know of no other religion with a hell for eternity. You see, the Christian tradition is ethically dualistic: there is a good God and a bad Devil, good people and bad people. The theological notion about hell is a perfectly good thing psychologically: if a person hangs on to his ego, and intentionally forbids his ego to be exalted by the fusion of something transcendent of this personal cycle, he has cut out

God's grace; he has cut out the saving power and will be in hell. But it's hard to get to hell, actually. According to the orthodox doctrine, it's only a mortal sin that will get you to hell; and a mortal sin must be a grievous matter, with sufficient reflection and full consent of the will. Well, there aren't many people who do that, and those who do ought to be in hell! [laughs] Otherwise, it's a venial sin. Even if you kill your mother in a passion, that's not sufficient reflection and full consent of the will. You may have a long, long session in Purgatory, according to the doctrine, but ultimately you have not excluded the grace of God.

Isn't there a line in the Gospel of Matthew, though, in which Christ refers to eternal hell fires?

I don't remember that passage. Also, what Christ said is not always what Jesus said. It's not always easy to be sure, because he spoke Aramaic and the texts are in Greek. And you know how the words of two languages so different don't quite match. Perhaps the Greek would tip over and say more than Jesus said, or less than he intended. For example, that little phrase about the kingdom of heaven being within you. I understand that in Aramaic there is what's called a potential present, which changes the structure of the sentence: the kingdom of heaven isn't within you, but it's *about to be* within you. Do you see? Then there is the question of the word "within," which can be interpreted as "within" or "among." So, is the kingdom of heaven within you, or is the kingdom of heaven about to be among you? The Aramaic might be read either way. There have been considerable arguments about that very crucial passage, because if the kingdom of heaven is within you, then God himself is within you because he's in the kingdom of heaven. Now, in the Thomas Gospel which has been translated out of the Coptic, it says specifically, definitely, and unquestionably that the kingdom of heaven is within, *in* you. And as I pointed out earlier, it also says that "the kingdom of the Father is spread over the earth and men do not see it."

That's a Buddhist notion really, isn't it, that the Mother Light is universal and we're excluding it from our own experience?

Yes. But then, Buddhism can actually spiritualize any religious tradition.

As practiced in Japan, Tibet, India, and Sri Lanka, there seem to be differences in Buddhism. What do they represent?

Well, just as Christianity is different in Western Europe and Eastern Europe, so Buddhism has adapted itself automatically to the understanding and mode of life of the people present. Buddhism went through an enormous transformation in the first century A.D. The earlier form of Buddhism, which is known as Theravada, also known as Hinayana, is a monastically oriented religion. The experience of Nirvana, it was thought, could not be fully realized except by cutting off the normal earthly way of living and moving into the monastic life.

Then, in the first century A.D., a reverse position was taken: in living the life of the world, you are *there*. Now that's the Buddhism of northwest India. That's the version that passed into China and Japan, whereas the earlier Buddhism was already established in Sri Lanka at the time of Ashoka and in Thailand, Cambodia, and Vietnam.

In Japan you find Buddhism in the arts, in flower arrangement, in the tea ceremony, and generally in the decorum of life. Although there are monks, they are not so greatly in evidence. There are two kinds of Buddhism in Japan today. One is the Buddhism of outside power, which has the image of the savior—for instance, Amida Buddhism—and it's through the mythology, the imagery, and prayers of that saving presence that you come to realization. Whereas in Zen, which is the other kind of Buddhism, you don't ask for a savior; you are your own savior. These two Buddhisms are very much alive in Japan.

In Tibet, on the other hand, there is a very strong emphasis on monastic Buddhism, on meditation, and on that enormous pantheon of different possibilities derived from different *sutras.*

Also prior to the arrival of Buddhism in Tibet, there was the Bon religion, which was the worship of nature spirits.

Well, the two interact. One characteristic of Buddhism, in contrast to Christianity, is that Buddhism does not eliminate deities. Rather, they are seen as manifestations of Buddha-consciousness in the mode of a given culture and are kept.

When the MacArthur people took a census of religious beliefs in Japan, they found that there were more religious believers than there were people, because everybody was both a Shinto and a Buddhist.

This capacity to accept other religions is based on a fundamental Buddhist belief that Buddha-consciousness is ubiquitous. The goal of Buddhism is to make the individual aware of the Buddha-consciousness in himself. Also, it accepts what the world produces and gives. I remember a Tibetan monk who had been in the Dalai Lama's palace at the time of the Chinese invasion. I was helping him with his autobiography. His teachers had been tortured; his friends had been killed; but I never heard a negative word about the Chinese from that man. It is all Buddha-process —the idea of what's called mutual arising: enemies arise mutually, and the situations are of a transcendent source. I learned from him what religion is; it's a perfectly beautiful thing.

That idea of acceptance is so far from our need to control.

That's the whole mystery: to have the mind submit. It must serve, not dominate, life. That's a major point in so many mythologies. The mind dominating life is really Satan, and life speaking through the mind is the power of the Christ. That's basic; that's the Buddha.

CHAPTER THREE

*M*ICHAEL: *Joseph, some people say we live in a time of transformation: throughout history, people have talked about living in a time of transformation.*

*J*OSEPH: There are certain periods when the transformation is quite special and extremely radical. And ours is certainly one of those periods. You must realize that the cultures of the world, since about 3000 B.C., have been mainly agrarian, and now are disintegrating under the impact of the industrial revolution. You must also realize that the early civilizations remained in relative isolation, with a controlled horizon within which people had essentially the same experiences. Now that those horizons are smashed, people of different beliefs and cultures are colliding with each other. The transformation is really of the whole sense of humanity and what it means to be a cultured and world-related human being. Anything from the past—such as an idea of what man of this, that, or another culture might be, or should be—is now archaic. And so we have to leave our little provincial stories behind. They may guide us as far as structuring our lives for the moment, but we must always be ready to drop them and to grab the new experience as it comes along, and to interpret it.

Why is it important for us to understand our past?

Well, as the saying goes, those who forget the past are condemned to repeat it. But more than that, there are certain motifs that continually recur, which can be recognized as a basic line of human spiritual need and potential. And the distractions of various moments of history may pull us away from that. It's through myth that you can, as it were, find your direct center line again. Plato, in the *Timaeus*, says that there's only one thing a man can do for another and that is to reintroduce him to those constant forms which at birth we lose track of because of the distractions of the senses.

Now, this is not to say that we must not be distracted by the senses; there's too rich a world, and there would be no history if we were not moving in different styles and different times. But this other, deeper line is a steadying thing. I found that the way to become really familiar with the various lines is by a comparative method: not remaining fixed in one mythological tradition—our own, for example—or getting excited about another and getting stuck with that. It amounts, really, to finding the spiritual norm of the human race. If you were to think of humanity only in terms of the structure of one or another of the various races of man, you would not have the whole picture. So it is when we become fixed to one mythological tradition, which until recently was the case. The story of ancient, medieval, and modern history is just one line. How many history books address only with vague references the great civilizations of India and China and Japan and the Muslim world, not to mention the non-literate societies? But these are also clues to basic human structuring functions.

There isn't much discussion of the spiritual ideals of these other cultures, either. How is that related to what's going on in the world politically?

In politics and economics, the mode inevitably is conflict. Politics is winning over somebody else; economics is, again, winning over somebody else. I think it's a good thing to have to fight, and to be in the world struggle; that's what life is. But it's in the spiritual realm that there are constants. It's a shame that typically there's been a fight in the spiritual realm also, namely, "Our religion is the true one, and these other people are pagans or infidels or whatnot," which is the political accent. The comparative approach, on the other hand, allows you to recognize the constants; it allows you to recognize that you are in counterplay—in your political and economic life—with one of your own kind, and you can regard the person as a "thou," as you would in a tennis game. You are no longer fighting a monster. But the old political style turns the man on the other side of the net into a monster. In every war we've done that. But to know that the other person is a "thou," a human being with the same sentiments and potentialities as yourself, at least civilizes the game. Then in other relationships there is the possibility of a real sense of accord and commonality.

What's before us now is the problem of our social group. What is it? Our social group is mankind. Formerly, it was this group or that. And in the older traditions, love was reserved for the in-group; aggression and all that was for others. There is no out-group now, so what are we going to do with the aggression? It has to be civilized.

Do you think politics can catch up?

I don't know what politics can do. I think it's fair to say that I'm a little bit discouraged by the people who are involved in the political life of this country. I begin to feel it has been betrayed. Its potentialities have been sold for values that are inscrutable to me.

One of the current aspects of life is the importance of technology. In your writings and in your lectures you've dealt with the ancient conflict between science and religion; in fact, you stated that it's really a conflict between 2000 B.C. and 2000 A.D. Do you now see a synthesis happening between religion and science?

My view is simply this. Our tradition has been rendered in scripture, and all of our institutional religions are based on that scripture, which dates from 2,000 or more years ago. As a result, we've become fixed to a view of the world that is out of accord with what we now are experiencing. Consider that in 1543, when Copernicus published his heliocentric system, it could not be assimilated by the religious teachers of the time. Likewise, in the middle of the nineteenth century, when Darwin brought out what was already a rather old theory of evolution—Goethe, among others, had proposed it—it was contrary to the idea of fixed species. As you say, the science that has been held against modern science is an archaic one, a fixed science of about 2000 B.C. against that of 2000 A.D. But any image can become an icon. And it seems to me that it's the work of poets and artists to know what the world-image of today is, and to render it as the old seers did theirs. The prophets rendered it as a manifestation of the transcendent principle. That's what we lack today, really. I think poets and artists who speak of the mystery are rare. There's been so much social criticism of our arts, which is just one facet. But the other function of the poet—that of opening the mystery dimension—has been, with few great exceptions, forgotten. I think that what we lack, really, isn't science but poetry that reveals what the heart is ready to recognize.

We don't seem to honor our artists and poets very much in our culture. Are there civilizations that do?

It's worse here in the United States. In France, they name streets after their poets; we have them named after generals. When you think of Melville, Mark Twain, and Emerson, and you go to the places where those men lived, there's no recognition of their having been there; names of former mayors are on five or six different street corners, but not the poets and the artists.

What does that reflect?

It reflects, I think, a businessman's mentality. That's what's running, and has run, and has made this country. It's a curiously unartistic country in its common character, and yet it has produced some of the greatest artists of the century. But they're not recognized publicly; those that are recognized publicly are the razzle-dazzlers who come across in the popular media.

People fatuitously fall on their faces before some marvelous movie actor, but the poet, the artist . . . And it isn't as though we didn't *have* poets and artists. For instance, Robinson Jeffers is one of the really great poets of the century; his "Roan Stallion," to me, is a revelation. And when I mention him, as I frequently do, people don't even know his name; but when they read the lines that I cite, they recognize a poet. It's curious.

We have few means to allow artists and poets to even survive in our culture.

One means of real support would be the popular mass media, and they're not interested.

Yes, because of the commercial orientation.

I don't know what it is. I don't understand those people. The things they're interested in purveying to the public seem to be of momentary sensational interest. I'm not saying that they're not worthy, but why are they all running in the same direction?

And you feel that it's important that art and poetry and music be a vital part of any culture.

It is what *is* vital; the rest isn't.

Joseph, in Myths to Live By, *you wrote:*

> . . . what we all today surely recognize is that we are entering—one way or another—a new age, requiring a new wisdom: such a wisdom, furthermore, as belongs rather to experienced old age than to poetically fantasizing youth, and which every one of us, whether young or

old, has now somehow to assimilate. Moreover, when we turn our thoughts to religion, the first and most obvious fact is that every one of the great traditions is today in profound disorder. What have been taught as their basic truths seem no longer to hold.

And I also want to cite a recent Gallup survey, which I think showed that there was a turning away from institutionalized religion, yet there is a tremendous surge in the search for the Ultimate.

There's an analogy to the present situation in the history of our American Indians in the nineteenth century. By the 1870s and '80s, the buffalo were wiped out so that the wheat fields of the advancing white man could develop and the iron horse wouldn't be interrupted, so that the food supply of the Indians would be removed and they'd have to go into reservations and accept the handouts of the United States government. As a result of that, the essential social religion which was centered on the buffalo began to disintegrate. The buffalo was the animal master and principal sacrificial victim—the one who was killed—and returned to the earth in ceremonies so that he could come again.

Part of Black Elk's vision, you remember, was the end of the buffalo age and the coming of the tree—the agricultural time. It was when the social religion dissolved and the object of the cult disappeared that the peyote cult came up from Mexico and overwhelmed the Plains cultures. With the outer object of vision and religious contemplation removed, the inward search began.

I think something like that is what has happened here. In the 1960s, there was a fundamental disillusionment about the political life in the United States; also, a disintegration of the religious position. Look at what happened to the Catholic Church with Vatican II—the turnover there was very unsettling. There is a turning inward. And I think it's that inward search that is dominant today. I recently received advertisements from the Roman Catholic Paulist Press for a series of books on Western mystics, that you couldn't find in bookstores. The advertisement said that the 1960s was for Oriental mysticism and the 1970s is going to be for the Western. The accent, you see, had been on institutional religion, and now, along comes what might be called the Pentecostal or inward experiential side—people like Dionysius the Areopagite, and Meister Eckhart, and John of the Cross. Well, here's an influence now accepted by an institution that traditionally has been a little disturbed about the mystical; because on the inward journey one comes in touch with the mysteries alone; whereas, traditionally, the institution has been officially the one purveyor of divine salvation.

And in athletics, all this mysticism of track, and the rapture and ecstasy in sexual experiences—all these are mystical; all related to the loss of ego and its tenacity—yielding to a larger opening. That's what mysticism is, and these are the foregrounds, these are the shallows of that depth.

A well-known statement is, "In wildness is the preservation of the world." In the city, nature is all but removed. Yet so much of mythology deals with the human connection with the earth, and with nature. Perhaps our environmental problems are partly due to the fact that we're out of touch with nature.

You have to realize first that the human being is a biological phenomenon himself. He's a product of nature. He has this body which is like the body of the grass or the tree: a product of this good earth. And, on the other hand, in contrast to the tree and the grass and the little bug, he has this great brain which has a structuring character that is not of nature. It has its own rational thinking of the mathematical kind. It is, let's say, rectangular, whereas corporal thinking is circular. These are the two kinds of consciousness that are in us. One is that which in India is called *Vijnanamayakosha*—the sheath of wisdom: the wisdom which digests our meals, which brings the grass up, and which we share with the whole world of nature. But then there's this *Manomayakosha*—this intelligence which has plans for how life should be, and it's not always the way life wants to be. So there's a conflict between these two worlds.

I think of it really in the way of the city, particularly of a city like New York. When the moon rises over those concrete canyons, it's an amazing sight. So the mind may be very well at home in New York, but this other support to the mind, which is our biology, is out of accord with that. And then you go out to the country and the body says: "Here's where I belong."

But the tendency in our culture is to be more of this mathematical organization, instead of the organic. And the interaction between these two is what keeps us civilized and harmonious human beings.

There are two things to be said. One, in wilderness is salvation. Yes. If that's wiped out, we're nothing but mechanical. The next thing, however, is that the whole function of myth is to unite these two orders of our nature: mental nature—the waking consciousness—and that thing which takes over in sleep. When people have nightmares, it's principally because they have been repressing the biology and it comes up with a vengeance. The deity that is disregarded turns into a devil. Nature becomes feared if it has been suppressed long enough and you are out of accord with it; it is always going to break up the quadrangular mode of planning that you've had for your life. Falling in love is nature coming in. And, my God, it has wrecked many a program! The nature-world is a wonderful thing to meet, but then we've got to have the other one, too.

Technology has sought to overcome nature and consequently there's an imbalance, if we look at other less industrialized countries.

Yes, and the irony of it all is that science really comes from paying attention to nature. It takes the possibilities of nature and recombines them; its basis is nature, too.

But there are two natures, really. Being in the air at 30,000 feet at sunset or at dawn, you realize there is a nature of these great physical phenomena. Then there is the nature of the trees and plants—the organic nature. And the nature our science is bringing in is the nature of the physical rather than the organic world.

How can we recover our connections with nature?

I think that's just a question of life planning. You should put yourself in a situation so that you will have that refreshment from time to time—even just taking a walk in the country on weekends or spending your holidays there. But if in your weekend or holiday you keep yourself in the world of enclosed civilized living, then the nature inside you becomes starved.

Those who seem happiest have a certain unity in their lives; work and leisure are integrated . . .

Well, again I can look at it only in terms of an individual. I think the person who takes a job in order to live—that is to say, for the money—has turned himself into a slave. *Work* begins when you don't like what you're doing. There's a wise saying: make your hobby your source of income. Then there's no such thing as work, and there's no such thing as getting tired. That's been my own experience. I did just what I wanted to do. It takes a little courage at first, because who the hell wants you to do just what you want to do; they've all got a lot of plans for you. But you can make it happen. I think it's very important for a young person to have the courage to do what seems to him significant in his life, and not just take a job in order to make money. But this takes a bit of prudence and very careful planning, and may delay financial achievement and comfortable living. But the ultimate result will be very much to his pleasure.

But there is an incredible amount of pressure to conform.

I know it. But there is a margin, too. There are plenty of ways to coast along until you find your center. I don't mean going on relief; I don't have much respect for people who expect society to support them while they're finding their feet. There are other ways to work that out. If you have a job, for instance, which allows you time enough to develop your own system of ideas for the future, and the boss offers you more money for extra hours, then you refuse that because it would take away from your free time. Do you see what I mean? Acceptance of the popular advancement is often to the detriment of your career work. Every artist has to make that kind of decision. If a writer says to himself, "Oh, I'll write pot-boilers until I get enough money to write," he's probably not going to write the book he wants to write when the time comes because he's learned to write pot-boilers. His hand is working from that level instead of from the higher one. So it's an early decision of courage to do the thing that's your authentic drive. That's the path where there's no path.

I don't know how it is today, but in the 1920s and '30s there were plenty of marginal areas where you could incubate your destiny. They must still exist.

We live in a society that really stresses the importance of materialistic security. When you look at other cultures and other mythologies, has this idea of security always been present?

I think the emphasis on security in our world is there because we have so much of it. Life is made pretty secure for us— so much so, in fact, that we forget what the dangers of life really are. We even have life insurance . . .

Paradoxical, isn't it?

There's no risk. On the other hand, there are so many examples of people today who have ventured the adventure. Wonderful people. And they are, you might say, counter-statements to this emphasis of the popular mind on security: tenure in the professions and all that kind of thing.

In a sense, it's jumping over the edge and moving into the adventure that really fires the creativity, don't you think?

I would say so. You don't have creativity otherwise.

One of the things that seems to have been lost to us is the presence of the hero. We constantly search for the person who's going to pull us out, be it the President or Superman. But the knight on the charger is not appearing as we supposed he would.

There are two aspects of the hero, I think. The hero is somebody whom you can lean on and who's going to rescue you; he is also an ideal. To live the heroic life is to live the individual adventure, really. One of the problems today is that with the enormous transformations in the forms of our lives, the models for life don't exist for us. In a traditional society— the agriculturally based city—there were relatively few life roles, and the models were there; there was a hero for each life role. But look at the past twenty years and what has come along in the way of new life possibilities and requirements. The hero-as-model is one thing we lack, so each one has to be his own hero and follow the path that's no path. It's a very interesting situation.

Or at least the models we tend to use are very strange ones. I think of Hollywood stars . . .

Oh, now those models come flashing in front of us and they *are* heroes of sorts. I think the athletic hero is right there. But these are bizarre kinds of heroes because they can't really be incorporated into one's life. Actors, personalities, politicians—they're mostly heroes in life-contexts that are not of the people who admire them. That's just a curious result of the fact that our society's changing so fast. But I think there are heroes—there's just no doubt about it. I think Martin Luther King was a hero. Kennedy was a hero—both Kennedys. And certain athletes.

They filled the model.

They filled the model. But they're not doing much for us in the way of helping us build our own lives. There are very few models for life. I think the individual has to find his own model. I found mine.

Isn't it important to respect our own uniqueness?

I think that's the most important thing of all. That's why, as I said, you really can't follow a guru. You can't ask somebody to give The Reason, but you can find one for yourself; you decide what the meaning of your life is to be. People talk about the meaning of life; there is no meaning of life—there are lots of meanings of different lives, and you must decide what you want your own to be.

Has this age of technology lost contact with that inner self?

To a large degree. People are now recovering it—at least people I know. But the nation is not recovering it. The wonderful thing about the Delphic Oracle, for example, was that governors and princes would go and ask the Oracle how to handle political affairs: and the advice from those centers isn't coming to us now. We've lost touch generally. People feel rootless because they have lost touch with those depths in their lives, and in our nation. Our nation is run by economics and politics; I find no spiritual goal in the decisions made today.

How do you think that happened?

Well, it's difficult to date. There is a general loss of confidence, and shame at what we've done and what we're doing in Third World countries. The people we have exploited, we now realize, have values and rights of their own. But this is an inevitable consequence of the last imperialistic stage of a culture. Rome faced the same thing—Virgil deals with this. And Goethe foresaw it in *Faust*; in the last act of Part II, Faust is in this period where ground-rooted people are uprooted and thrown aside so that housing developments can be built, and all that kind of thing.

It struck me very strongly in Egypt when I visited Aswan.

When the dam was built there, the water backed up and wiped out the whole province of Nubia. What happened to the Nubians? They were moved out and put in housing developments. In *Faust*, Act V—that's exactly what's happening there. There's a kind of inevitability about it. Nobody's to blame: the culture moves from a deep spiritual impulse, a lyric moment that creates the forms of the culture, to more pragmatic considerations.

Well, I find the same thing in my own personal life. As I grow older, more and more economic and political details keep pushing in, and I wonder what became of that early inner quietness that allowed me to move out of my own center. This is just perhaps an organic process of moving from the lyric of childhood to the practical problems of later life.

We have the institution without spiritual values. At the same time there are movements, obviously of great value: ecology, women, equal rights, peace. How do those movements relate to those decaying institutions?

What's happened to the institutions is that they have become self-interested rather than of service to a national impulse. So people break away. There are various spiritual aims, but they don't coordinate into something that supports the whole. They become revolutionary and really destructive. The old things are falling apart, and the new things are showing themselves. There are inklings here and there—twinklings around some great fire that eventually will have a positive, creative power to it.

Is there a historical example we might compare ourselves to?

Well, again, the Roman world might be one. It covered an enormous territory and incorporated a great many peoples into one culture. Finally, it disintegrated as different groups took over. In the South, Islam came out of that same domain;

and in the North, the European culture-world. In the Northeast, the Russian culture was beginning. So there was a disintegration. But what's happening here, I think, is actually the opposite: many cultures are pouring into one great domain and are having a hard time.

So there's still fragmentation.

And there's going to be for a long time. Unfortunately, many of the new mystically motivated movements are reactionary against other peoples. We have this "Power" and that "Power" and the other "Power." These are delaying actions. People are afraid to move into the free fall of a totally new way of looking at others. So the new mythology to come must be a global mythology, and it's got to solve the problem of the in-group by showing that there's no out-group. We're all members of a society of the planet, not of one particular place, and the fact that the three main religions of the Western world—Judaism, Christianity, and Islam—can't live together in Beruit is a refutation of all three in terms of their value for the contemporary world. They're monstrous! We must begin to realize that each is saying in his own language what the other is trying to say in his. There must be brotherhood and cooperation. Because unless that comes, we're going to blow ourselves to smithereens.

Every single one of the old horizon-bound mythologies reserved love for the in-group, and aggression and denigration were reserved for the out-group. Now, something's got to break that. And when we see that picture of our planet taken from the moon, the question arises: What are we going to do with our aggression? How is it going to be absorbed into love and transmuted from gross matter to gold? I think teaching "I-thou" relationships, rather than the "I-it" relationships, which Buber spoke about, is the first step. The teaching of *humanity* rather than the teaching of in-group appreciations is what's important.

The recognition of our connection with other peoples is vital.

But I see people pulling back into in-group associations. Just look all around you. This group, that group, the other: "We're It." And the challenge of the day of opening out to humanity is being ducked because it means giving up what we have and are sure of. We feel comfortable with our close friends, and uncomfortable with people who might have totally different thoughts. We are afraid to un-shell.

The challenge for the present and the future is to try to build bridges even though that may be difficult.

Yes. The big challenge, however, is education—an inner education so that the person identifies himself with humanity rather than with the in-group. Now, that isn't easy, because "humanity" is a vague concept, and the in-group is what you're experiencing, and love and anxieties come from person-to-person relationships. I think the actual transfer of people from round about is good. In a New York subway, you see every race in the world! Except now, each of those races is asking for its own in-group advantages over the others.

Do you see hope in any of the movements that have emerged over the last few decades?

Yes, I do. On my lecture tours, I've met beautiful people who hold out great hope and expectation. You see, when the world seems to be falling apart, stick to your own trajectory; hang onto your own ideals and find kindred spirits. That's the rule of life. And it's that life that survives the megadeath.

So there's another side to the darkness.

Yes. Spengler has an image of the ideal when all's falling apart: he says it's the soldier in Pompeii who stayed right at his post when the volcanic ash was coming down. Even at the worst moment, if you are holding on to your trajectory, you've won. It's those who get thrown off track who are lost.

Perhaps the loss of vision is the result of a much smaller world. We know what happens on the other side of the planet, practically within seconds. And cultures are breaking down in the sense that national boundaries are no longer as rigid as they once were.

Well, Michael, I think you've addressed the real crux of the problem. Every mythology—and a mythology is an organizing system that holds a culture together—evolved within a bounded horizon of experience and intention. Now all these bounding horizons are broken.

When I was a boy, you never saw a Hindu in the United States. Today, within thirty hours you can be in India. And it's normal to see young people from the Orient on our campuses. So ideas are pouring back and forth into the various cultures that had never been operative in their lives before.

Now, among other things, mythology deals with a culture context. One of its functions is to validate and maintain a certain culture system; and these cultures are in transformation within themselves. At the same time, in meeting other cultures, you are reared back to your own. You can ask, "What is my society? What is my in-group?" Then you know your myth.

Well, the only in-group that's proper for today is the planet, and there's an enormous challenge to open up to that; to give not only yourself but your culture to the planetary view. But you see people pulling back into in-groups which have a long tradition of self-preservation. We don't have the universal social image yet.

If we go through history—and you're an ideal person to take that journey with—we see conflicts and wars, religious and otherwise—such terrible destruction. But there are some

*who say, "Well, it's human nature to fight; war will be with us
as long as we are human beings." How do you see that?*

Well, I think historically that's not quite true. There were
village raids in primitive cultures. And then there are some
peoples who just like to fight! They realize they can get things
by plundering those who can't fight as well as they can. But the
real systematic development of civilized warfare began very
soon after the rise of the first cities in Mesopotamia. The first
texts celebrating conquest—not just raiding and then running
off, but taking the land, taking the city—appear at the time of
Sargon I, about 2350 B.C. Those texts raise your hair when you
read them. They tell how he slew the people of this city and
that, north, south, east, and west; and this terrible refrain at
the end: "And I washed my weapons in the sea." And that's the
beginning of "civilized" warfare.

There are two kinds of warfare. One is this imperialistic
knocking down the neighbor and washing your weapons in
the sea; and the other is the kind we read of in the Book of
Judges and in Joshua: a bunch of Bedouin nomads come
raiding down on a city. That happened full scale in the third
and second millenniums B.C. The Indo-Europeans came down
from the North; the Semites came raiding out of the Seiro-
Arabian desert. Walls were built around cities, but they
couldn't stand up against those raiding forces.

*Are there peoples in the past who exhibited a peaceful as
opposed to a warlike nature?*

The people of the first towns and cities were basically peaceful people. They were agricultural people and peace was very
important for them. The suffering of war on their part was
from the invasions of nomadic, herding people who liked a
good fight. And the first signs of impingement by those warrior
people on the early cities is seen in the defensive walls that were
raised against them. The city people wanted peace.

What would happen after a city fell was that the conqueror, who had been a nomad, now as master would start the imperial war. Sargon I was of an invading race and wanted war.

But the people themselves—the peasants—were basically peaceful.

Are there any mythologies of peace?

The mythology of peace comes in the doctrines of Jesus, or Lao Tzu, or the Buddha. But those do not dominate the culture. Spengler has a statement in *The Decline of the West* which stays in my mind: "If you haven't the courage to be the hammer, you'll be in the role of the anvil." And that's just the ABCs of political life.

You've written about the idea that myth has been lost to us. Do you think that the various cultures imported from all over had something to do with the fact that this mixture of the different traditions produced a kind of "no-myth" society?

The founding myth of the United States was the Christian myth, in one sectarian form or another. Every state in the Northeast was formed by a sect that departed from the one next door, but these were all variants of the Christian tradition, which saw the truth as uniquely present in Christianity. There was an actual degradation and denial of the possibility that any other might be just as valid, so that the deities of the Indians and their divine experiences were regarded as diabolical manifestations. I think that was a terrible thing to have happened. It lead to near-extinction of the Native American cultures here.

Also you can see it in ordinary things like our roads. These ribbons of concrete running across the continent—and I've driven across it many, many times—allow you to just pass through it; you don't absorb the country. The people who moved into it established a relationship to the land by themselves. They don't have any tradition to help them.

I think that the movement towards respect for the land

represents a renewed realization that this is our land, that we can't violate it without violating our own lives, that we must love it and deal with it on its terms. It may be too late, however; I don't know.

Does the disappearance of the nuclear family and the loss of ancestral heritage have any bearing on the matter? We seem to be a society of individuals.

There, you see where we are. We're between two worlds: one world that is dissolving right around us, and the other to come that hasn't shown its full features yet. The nation is something that is going to have to dissolve, but not the family unit; the family unit is an organic base. A lot of our troubles come from the dissolution of the family—everything has been thrown onto the schools. We receive children who haven't learned how to behave decently as human beings, and it's supposed to be up to the schools to inculcate ethics; that lies behind this whole prayer-in-the-school problem. Prayer should be at home because there are so many different prayer systems. Having children listen to prayers recited to a deity who may not be the deity of their family is throwing the whole thing out of order. The family has to assume the responsibility, and I don't know how it can be brought about that when people commit themselves to having children, it's also their job to make sure their offspring grow up to be decent human beings.

And in our transitional society, what will be the role of myth? You said it must pull the world together.

That, too. But the role of myth will be what it has always been: to render in contemporary terms the mysteries of our own inner life, and the relationship of these mysteries to the cosmic life—because we are all parts of the cosmos. So myth has got to deal with the human system in relation to the mystery of the universe.

CHAPTER FOUR

*M*ICHAEL: *Joseph, how did you become interested in mythology?*

*J*OSEPH: I'd have to say it was due to having been brought up a Roman Catholic, and having taken it very seriously as a boy. Then my father used to take me to see Buffalo Bill when he brought his Wild West shows to Madison Square Garden, which was exciting. And we used to go to the Museum of Natural History, where I was tremendously impressed by the great room full of totem poles. My father was very generous in helping me find books about the American Indians—George Bird Grinnell's books, Indian Lodge Tales, the reports of the American Bureau of Ethnology, and so on. I eventually became a sort of little walking scholar in the field of American Indians.

Meanwhile, I was being educated by the nuns in the Roman Catholic religion and it didn't take me very long to realize that there were virgin births, deaths and resurrections, in both mythological systems. So very early on I became interested in this comparative realization, and by the age of eleven or twelve, I was pretty well into the material.

Then, in my university years, I specialized in the literature of the Middle Ages—the Arthurian romances and so forth—and, supporting that, of course, the classical mythologies.

Again I found the same images in a context of the Christian tradition, and yet inflected toward the more universal point of view.

You studied in Europe for a time.

Yes. My graduate work in Medieval literature took me to France and Germany. In Paris, I found modern art which dealt with the same themes—Picasso is full of them, for example; Klee is also a marvelous source. Then of course there was James Joyce, whose work I've spent a long time studying. He was one who helped me to see how symbols and myths are put together.

Much of your work is focused on the East and its philosophies and spiritual traditions. How did you become interested in that area?

Well, by chance, I met Jiddu Krishnamurti on a steamer to Europe, back in 1924. He was traveling with his friend Raj Gopal, and his brother, Nitya, who died the next year. There was also a young woman with him, and she gave me a copy of Edwin Arnold's *Light of Asia*, which is the life of the Buddha. Then, after a year in Paris, doing research on Medieval material, I went to Germany, where I discovered Thomas Mann— who was also incorporating myths into his work. I read Freud and Jung for the first time there, too. But I went to Germany really to study philology—the history of language—and this brought me to Sanskrit, and from that point the whole world of the Orient opened up. There were all those symbols again. Long years later, after I had been teaching and writing, I met Heinrich Zimmer, the great Indologist and a genius with respect to the interpretation of symbols. To my mind, he is supplementary to Jung. They were close friends during the last years of Zimmer's life. In fact, Jung edited Zimmer's German posthuma, as I edited Zimmer's American lectures which sent me deeply into the Orient. So when I finally met Jung we were co-editors, which was nice. But those two men are the ones who spoke to me. Also, at the same time that I was editing Zimmer, I was helping Swami Nikhilananda edit and translate the *Upanishads* and *The Gospel of Sri Ramakrishna*. And I knew Coomaraswamy and his work. So all this just opened out into vast, vast reaches.

Joseph, you said that Jung also has an effect on your work. Could you talk about that?

When I was a graduate student in Germany—this was in 1928–29—I discovered the works of Freud and Jung, which opened up a psychological dimension to the field of mythology. Suddenly I realized why the subject was interesting to me, and a lot of new mysteries and wonders came through.

Now, Jung was not known very well in the United States at that time. I think there were two small translations of his work. Freud, of course, was well known. Only I had not been a student of psychology, so both of these men began to inform me about one aspect of my own subject. I now saw that one aspect of the subject is the psychological mystery and the other aspect is historical and ethnographical. So, on the psychological side, these two men played back and forth in my thinking. When I wrote *The Hero with a Thousand Faces*, they were equal in my thinking: Freud served in one context, Jung in another. But then, in the years following, Jung became more and more eloquent to me. I think the longer you live, the more Jung can say to you. I go back to him every so often, and things that I've read before always say something new. Freud never says something new to me anymore; Freud tells us what myths mean to neurotics. On the other hand, Jung gives us clues as to how to let the myth talk to us in its own terms, without putting a formula on it. So I've been with Jung since 1928, and that's a long spell. As I say, he brings more and more to me. But he's not the final word—I don't think there is a final word; his work has opened up prospects and vistas, however.

You met Carl Jung. What was he like as a person?

Oh, he was a magnificent man. And he was no Herr Doktor Professor—we didn't talk about subjects in which he was an authority; we were ad-libbing. That was fun. Jean and I had tea with him and his wife at Bollingen—in that marvelous little castle he built with his own hands, on the lake near Zurich. He was a big man, and my wife tells me that his eyes were very attractive.

In your studies of mythology, have you found anything to verify the idea of the collective unconscious?

What are you going to do with the fact that the same motifs appear everywhere? There's a constellation of motifs that are fundamental. How do you explain it? Myths come from the same zone as dreams, so that individual dreams won't be alike. But here we come to a level of what might be called racial dreams—the myths—and they match, they match, they match. The term "collective unconscious," or general unconscious, is used in recognition of the fact that there is a common humanity built into our nervous system out of which our imagination works. The appeal of these constants is very deep.

Now, the explanation that is often given in Freudian circles of individual experiences being the source of dream biography, and different racial histories being the source of their myth, is inadequate. That won't explain it! It doesn't fit. It may say something about a certain inflection or aspect of this mythology as compared with that one. Why does this group see themselves as the special people, though a group over there doesn't think that way—their deities have to do with the world of nature? What is it that gives those different pitches to the different culture systems—not special history and biography—but what about the general humanity? You can recognize a human being no matter where you see him. He must have the same kind of basic nervous system, therefore his imagination must work out of a comparable base. What's so damn mystical about all that? That seems to me to be obvious. And that's what the term "collective unconscious" covers.

Jungian psychology seems to be more open than other more traditional forms of interpretation.

You know, for some people, "Jungian" is a nasty word, and it has been flung at me by certain reviewers as though to say, "Don't bother with Joe Campbell; he's a Jungian." I'm not a Jungian! As far as interpreting myths, Jung gives me the best clues I've got. But I'm much more interested in diffusion and relationships historically than Jung was, so that the Jungians think of me as a kind of questionable person. I don't use those formula words very often in my interpretation of myths, but Jung gives me the background from which to let the myth talk to me.

If I do have a guru of that sort, it would be Zimmer—the one who really gave me the courage to interpret myths out of what I knew of their common symbols. There's always a risk there, but it's the risk of your own personal adventure instead of just gluing yourself to what someone else has found.

Is there any current literature that deals with mythology?

I haven't been reading any of the most recent works. When I was shaping my own life-views, there were a number of authors that meant a great deal to me; but I don't know if they are still in the wind. One, as I said, was James Joyce. *A Portrait of the Artist as a Young Man* and *Ulysses* were two formative books for me. And along with them—saying the same thing in another language—were the works of Thomas Mann. They meant a lot to me as well. *The Magic Mountain*, I must say, was tremendous. In the world of poetry, W. B. Yeats has the messages; and so does T. S. Eliot, in a somewhat more stilted way. I feel that he knew about them but didn't feel them quite the way these other men did. Robinson Jeffers here on the West

Coast, and Walt Whitman on Long Island—these are people who continually refresh me.

In one of your books you discussed Joyce's Ulysses *and said that your first reaction to it was one of confusion. How did you eventually learn the symbology of that book?*

Well, I was in Paris at that time [1927]. Joyce was not known in this country. *Ulysses* wasn't permitted here, and we had no idea that he had already begun work on the wild thing that was to become *Finnegans Wake*. So I went into a bookstore, and there was *Ulysses* in its blue cover. I got a copy and started reading. But by chapter three I was going crazy. I went around to Shakespeare and Company, the publisher, on Place de l'Odéon, and I walked in, an indignant academic. "How do you read a thing like this?" And Sylvia Beech said, "As follows." And she gave me some information and books to help me on my way.

But, talking about innovation—is that book not an innovation! Every single chapter is a totally new innovation; there's no repetition of anything; and this moves right on through *Finnegans Wake* in grand style.

You discovered something in Finnegans Wake *regarding Nixon. What was that?*

I found that Watergate was a re-run of *Finnegans Wake*. I had worked for four years on *Finnegans Wake*, and then as Watergate was developing, it seemed to be more and more reminiscent of something. Then, one fine day, it dawned on me: "It's *Finnegans Wake*!" *Finnegans Wake*, to put it very briefly, is the nightmare of a political man whose career is being undone by rumor. A hen in a neighboring yard has dug up, out of a mud mound, a letter which would disclose all the necessary facts. But wherever a significant phrase occurs, it has been punctured by the hen's beak. The newspaper reporters are out interviewing every dog in the street about what his opinion is, and publishing these things in yards and yards of reports. There are four drooling old men who give you their instant analyses of everything that has happened. And I think you know who they are.

The TV channels.

Very solid citizens reviewing a whole lot of evidence. No one knows quite what happened and the witnesses who were drunk are—if anyone is responsible—responsible also. And so it goes on unfolding. Every now and then you hear the voice of the politician himself, whose initials are H.C.E., meaning Here Comes Everybody. His voice comes forth telling of the great things he's done for humanity, and his wife abuses all his critics, and so on. He shows that all of us are, in a sense, both guilty and worthy of compassion. This is his view of the human race, which he loves. The wonderful thing about this book is that there is no judgment.

That's wonderful, Joseph. You once said you have to risk in order to find life, that so often people go into work thinking of making money instead of looking for something that will inspire them to life action. Have you ever done anything in your life primarily for money?

No. Absolutely not. I would have, I think, but I came back from Europe about two weeks before the crash, and I didn't have a real job for five years. But I found—I don't know whether it would work now—that a young unmarried man didn't need much money; I could take care of myself pretty well for almost nothing. My decision to follow this course came one day in Paris while I was sitting in the little garden of Cluny, where the Boulevards St. Michel and St. Germain come together. It suddenly struck me: What in heaven's name am I doing? I don't even know how to eat a decent, nourishing meal, and here I'm learning what happened to vulgar Latin when it passed into Portuguese and Spanish and French. So I dropped work on the Ph.D. On my return, I found a place in upstate New York and read the classics for twelve hours a day. I was enjoying myself enormously, and realized I would never finish my degree because it would have required me to do things that I had already outgrown. In Europe, the world had opened up: Joyce, Sanskrit, the Orient, and the relationship of all these to psychology. I couldn't go back and finish up that Ph.D thesis; besides, I didn't have the money. And that free-wheeling, maverick life gave me a sense of the deep joy in doing something meaningful to me.

When, after five years, I was invited to teach at Sarah Lawrence College, I found that they were very excited by what I wanted to do. I would not have taken a job otherwise, just as I wouldn't take the Ph.D. I don't know how it would have been had I been married with a child. I can't speak to that point. But it wasn't by accident that I wasn't married because it was my notion that before a commitment like that, I should be prepared to take care of the situation.

You have been married for some forty years now—

Forty-six years [1984].

—to Jean Erdman. During that time, we've gone from a traditional patriarchal ideal of woman to the feminist movement and the assertion of women's power—a return of the goddesses, if you will. What's happening in these changes of the past couple of decades?

We're in a marvelous moment with respect to the state of women, and it's a moment just as crucial for men because the archetypology of just the wife and mother is gone. Many a man, when he thinks of marriage, imagines that archetype, and he is unwilling or unable to face the fact of a female personality. Men have had a wider range of life courses enabling them to develop their potentials, but women have been condemned to one style, one system of interests and concerns.

That's not true anymore; the world has opened up to them. Now there are very few models for them. The immediate model is the men's world, and many women move into that in competition.

But the great thing is the emerging possibility of the female personality as the guiding image of the woman's own life. And then her husband has to match that. He's in dialogue now with an unpredictable presence, because the sexes are deeply mysterious to each other—really and wonderfully so.

You see, the whole thing in marriage is the relationship and yielding—knowing the functions, knowing that each is playing a role in an organism. One of the things I have realized—and people who have been married a long time realize—is that marriage is not a love affair. A love affair has to do with immediate personal satisfaction. But marriage is an ordeal; it means yielding, time and again. That's why it's a sacrament: you give up your personal simplicity to participate in a relationship. And when you're giving, you're not giving to the other person: you're giving to the relationship. And if you realize that you are in the relationship just as the other person is, then it becomes life building, a life fostering and enriching experience, not an impoverishment because you're giving to somebody else. Do you see what I mean?

This is the challenge of a marriage. What a beautiful thing is a life together as growing personalities, each helping the other to flower, rather than just moving into the standard archetype. It's a wonderful moment when people can make the decision to be something quite astonishing and unexpected, rather than cookie-mold products.

Do you think the high divorce rate comes from failure to recognize that?

Partly. And to be able to continue the adventure. Because no matter whom you tie your life to, you're going to find the person mysterious. There will be a lot that you didn't know about, and even the person himself didn't know about. And remember, the person is having the same problem in relation to you.

And both are changing all the time.

All the time.

So often we want to freeze the other person into a position.

Naturally. People have a notion of what a marriage ought to be, and the marriage that they want. You can't have that and have the adventure of a love marriage. It's got to be one or the other. And wherever love takes you, there you are.

And that's the adventure.

That *is* the adventure! I see marriage in two stages. One is that wonderful impulse stage of youth where everything is "coming up roses" and the birds are singing and all that. Then there comes a time when those vital energies aren't there, but at the same time there is an awakening of a spiritual relationship. When that doesn't happen, you see people getting divorced. I've been shocked at the number of my friends who brought up a family, everything seems wonderful, the kids are gone, and they get divorced!

You know the story about the priest, the minister, and the rabbi who ask when life begins? The priest says, "It begins at conception." The minister says, "Oh, it begins after twenty days or something like that." And the rabbi says, "It begins when the children have graduated and the dog has died." And that's just the time when people tend to grow apart. They all need things that bond them together, the physical things—the joy of bringing up the family. And with all that gone, what next?

In some sense, too, all those things have become walls to prevent us from really asking the question "Why am I here?"

Yes.

What's it all about?

You've got a lot of reasons just to have two cars, you know? Win the lottery, or something like that, but for heaven's sake, what's the adventure? And it gets to be more and more adventurous the longer you live. I can tell you that much!

I'd believe it, Joseph, coming from you. It has to be true!

[Joseph laughs]: You'll get there, Michael.

INDEX

A

A Vision 74
Aion 61
Albertus Magnus 81
alchemy 80–82
Alexandria 91
Apocalypse 79
Apollo 51
Ashoka 91
Aquinas, Saint Thomas 81–82, 94
Arabian Nights, The 26
archetypal idea and local inflection 47–48, 51, 59–60, 63–64, 68
arts, function of 22, 102–103
ascension to heaven, cf. physics 77–78
Atlantis 40–42
Aurora Consurgens 82
Avalokiteshvara 43
avatars 94
Aztec 45, 46 (*see also* Mayan-Aztec)

B

Bastian, Adolf 51, 68
Beech, Sylvia 124
Bible
gospel of Matthew 57–58
literal vs. symbolic interpretation of 57, 58, 67, 82
birds, myth of two 58

Birth of Tragedy, The 51
Black Elk 34, 39, 104
Black Elk Speaks 34
"blasphemy," god within labelled as 84–85
Blackfoot Indians 83
bliss *see* "following your bliss"
Bodhisattva 58
Jesus as 91
Bon religion 97
Brahman, Saguna/Nirguna 55
Buber, Martin 112
Buddha 91, 96, 97, 116, 120
as Prince Five Weapons 29
Buddha-consciousness 91, 97
Buddha-process 97
Buddhism 96–97
Amida 96
Hinayana and Mahayana 56–57
Tibetan (pantheon) 92
Zen 66, 96
buffalo, end of age of 34, 104

C

Call, the
and morphology of experiences 25–26
as essence of mythology 23
missing 27
refusal of 23, 25
sense of 24
when it occurs 27
camel, lion, dragon as spiritual symbols 75–76

Campbell, Joseph, background
of see Chapter 4
Campbell, Jean Erdman 122,
126
challenge for present and
future 101–102, 113, 114
Chandogya Upanishad 85
Chartres 61, 62, 71
Chavín 49
child, becoming as a 75–76
China
and Mayan-Aztec
culture 42, 43
Shang dynasty 40
Christ
power of the 97
-principle 94
"Christ Triumphant" 91
Christianity
and vision quest 31
concept of God in 55
crux of 39
Devil in 29
ethically dualistic 94
sanctioned by Roman
Empire 60
city, shift in focal point of 71–
72
collective unconscious 122–
123
and mythology 50
vs. diffusion 43, 49
commonalities 52
commonalty 53
comparative method 99, 100,
101
consciousness, two kinds 105–
106
Cooke, Thomas Cardinal 63

Coptic writings 62, 95
compassion 53
Cortez, Hernando 46
cosmos as mountain 42
cross, as symbol 45, 69
Crucifixion 58, 68–69
cults 70–72

D

Dalai Lama, H.H. the
XIVth 63, 64
Dante Alighieri 56
Dead Sea Scrolls 62
death 78
death and resurrection 60–61,
77, 119
demons
as limitations 28
"Sticky Hair" 29
why we repress 30–31
departure 46
desī 68, 70
devil 51, 84
as a god not
recognized 28–29, 106
as obsession in
Christianity 29
diffusion
and collective
unconscious 43, 48, 49
East-West 40–45
Dionysus 51
Divine Comedy 56
Don Juan (in Carlos Castenada
novels) 37–38
dragon of "Thou shalt" 75–76

E

Eckhart, Meister 55, 56, 88
education 113

elementary ideas 68
Eliot, T.S. 33, 123
von Eschenbach, Wolfram 32–33
eternity 69, 78
ethics and religion 86
ethnic ideas 68
Euhemeristic theory 48

F

family unit 117
Faust 110–111
Finnegans Wake 124–125
flood motif 67–68, 83–84
Floris, Joachim of 62
"following your bliss" 24
    and money 25, 107–108, 125–126
    as left-hand path 31
folk ideas 48, 68
Fool (defined) 39–40
Francis, Saint 62
Freud, Sigmund 50, 120, 121
Freudian interpretation of dream, myth 122

G

Gimbutas, Marija 41
Gnosticism 62, 77, 90
God
    as female 40–41, 52
    as male 40–41, 52
    as personality 55
    beyond "God" 55, 56, 88
    concept of 55, 88
    within 58–59, 64, 79, 89, 92
    within, labelled as "blasphemy" 84–85

The Gods and Goddesses of Old Europe 41
Goethe, Johann Wolfgang von 102, 110
Gospel According to Thomas 57, 62, 70, 90, 95
Govinda, Lama (*The Way of the White Clouds*) 93
Grail, quest of
    as essence of Western spirituality 73
    different versions 32–33, 73
    hero of 33
    meaning of 33–34
Grof, Stanislav 50
Guede 94, 95
guru *see* teacher-disciple relationship

H

Heine-Geldern, Robert 43
heaven, kingdom of 95
Hell 67, 94–95
Hermes 77, 80–81
Hermetic tradition 76–77, 80–82
    and Mosaic doctrine 77
Hermes Trismegistus 77
Hero (*see also* Trickster, Fool)
    as model 59, 109
    defined 23, 65
    formula for deification of historical 46, 48–49
    grail 65
    historical figure vs. cosmological principle 38–39, 46
    savior 60

Hero with a Thousand Faces, The 23, 121
  "The Refusal of the Call" 23, 25
Heyerdal, Thor 41
Holy Land as here and now 32
hunting vs. planting/gathering cultures 51–52

I

Idea of Man 36
immigration, effects of on U.S.A. 87, 112, 113
Intimations of Immortality 27
Ishtadevata 93
Isis 77
"I-thou" relationships 63, 86, 101, 112

J

Jeffers, Robinson 103, 123
Jesus 70, 116
  and Christ-principle 94
  as Bodhisattva 91
  as Hero 59
  as inspiration to life of spirit, awakener 26
  as second Person of Blessed Trinity 39
  as sole savior 39
  "Christ Triumphant" 91
  "Dread the passage of . . ." explained 26–27
  implications of resurrection of 84
  Second Coming of 57
Joachim of Floris 62
Joseph and His Brothers 83

Joyce, James 120, 123, 124
Jung, C.G. 50, 120, 121, 122
Jungian psychology 123

K

Kennedy, John F. and Robert F. 109
King, Martin Luther 109
kingdom of heaven within/among, in Aramaic 95
Krishnamurti, Jiddu 120
Kukulcán 38, 45, 48

L

Laing, R.D. 50
land, respect for the 116–117
Lemuria 40
life
  loyalty to 53
  when it begins 128
lion, as symbol in Nietzsche 75–76

M

male-female dominance in cultures 51–52
male god principle 40–41
Mann, Thomas 83, 120, 123
marga 68
marriage 74, 126–128
Masks of God, The 44, 51
Mass, Roman Catholic 68–70
Mayan-Aztec architecture, parallels to 42
Mayan-Aztec culture
  and China 42, 43
  and Egypt 41
  and Mesopotamia 42
meditation, function of 57

Mithraism 61
Mormon Church 71
Mosaic symbols 77
Moses 38, 77
mother goddess principle 52
movements, reactionary 111–113, 114
mystic, neophyte 79–80
Mythic Image, The 43, 45, 49, 59, 61
mythologically grounded life, two ways of living 23–24
Myths to Live By 103–104
myth(ology)
    and commonalities 52, 114
    and stages of life 32
    arises from life system, not concept system 21
    as energy-evoking sign 22
    as expression of collective unconscious 50, 122
    as great poems expressing insight 22, 23, 34–35
    as life-shaping image 35
    as meeting of psychological and metaphysical 21–22
    as sudden insight 22
    as system of analogies 81
    common vocabulary of images at base of 60
    enactment in ritual 34–35, 68–69
    function of 106, 114
    Freudian interpretation of 122
    how Campbell became interested in 119
    its song 63–64
    major point of 52, 97

modern role of 117
of peace 116
points beyond fact 21
new, must be global 112, 114

N

Navaho 38, 59
Neihardt, John (*Black Elk Speaks*) 34
Nietzsche, Friedrich Wilhelm 51, 56, 75–76
Nirvana 56, 57, 96
nondual realization 56–57

O

Olmec 40, 49
Olympics 35–36
Osiris 48, 59

P

Padmasambhava 29
Palenque 45
Parzival 33
Parzival 33
past, importance of understanding the 99–100
Paul, Saint 39, 59
peace, mythologies of 116
peyote cult 104
Pizarro, Francisco 46
Plato
    Critias 40
    Timaeus 40, 100
poets, function of 102
politics 86, 100–101
possession 93–94
pottery 43, 44

prayer 117
psyche, as cave with jewels 26

Q

Queste del Saint Graal, La 33, 73
Quetzalcoatl 38, 45, 47, 48

R

Ramakrishna, Sri 55, 64, 66
religion
  and cultism 70–72
  and science 101–102
  contemporary, "in a bad spot" 84
  contrasted with ethics, morality, politics 86
  Eastern, impact on Western culture 55–56, 64, 65, 70, 88–90
  favorite Campbell definition of 78
  "high" 59
  organized, and alchemy 81–82
  symbols in *see* symbols
Rig Veda 58
ritual, as enactment of myth 34–35, 68–69

S

saints *see under individual names*
Salt Lake City 71
salvation, individual vs. institutional 60–61, 62, 81, 85, 89, 110
Samsara 56
Sargon I 115, 116
Satan 97

sat-chit-ananda 78
Savior, one or many 60–61
Schopenhauer
  on life as planned 24–25
  on spontaneous compassion 53
second coming 46, 47, 57
shaman
  and priest, compared 28, 37
  importance of role of 36–37
  problem of 27
Silesius, Angelus 90
Sons of Light vs. Sons of Darkness 62
space, womb of 61
Spengler, Oswald 113, 116
spirit
  ideal for West 85–86, 90
  stages, in Indian tradition 85
  three stages of in Joachim of Floris 62
  three stages of in Nietzsche 75–76
spirituality
  and individual quest 90–91
  essence of Western 73–74
"Sticky Hair" 29
surrender 92
symbols
  as vehicles between conscious and unconscious 78, 81
  literal vs. spiritual reading of 57, 58, 66, 67–68, 77, 78–79, 83
  Mosaic vs. Hermetic interpretation 77

taken as referents in
contemporary religion 84
Symbols of Transformation 50
synchronicity 47
synthesis, East-West 88–90

T

Tammuz 48
teacher-disciple
relationship 72–75, 89–90,
123
temple, importance of 71
Temple of Inscriptions, figure
in 45–46
Theodosius I 60, 89
Thera 40
Thus Spake Zarathustra 75
Toynbee, Arnold Joseph 26
"transparent to
transcendence" 22, 70, 85
Thoth 77
trajectory, holding on to
one's 34, 113–114
transference 75
tree of life 58
Trickster, trickster hero 29,
39, 48 (*see also* Fool)
Trinity 39, 78
de Troyes, Chrétien 32

U

unity, levels of 52
Ulysses 123, 124
Upanishads 31

V

Vatican II 104

vision quest, the 23
and demons 28–29
counterpart in Christian
mythology 31
defined 27–28
Viracocha 47, 48
virgin birth 46, 60, 77, 82,
119
defined 23
voodoo 93

W

war 115–116
Waste Land 66, 67
defined 33, 65
Waste Land, The (T.S.
Eliot) 33
Watergate 124
Whitman, Walt 124
"way of the village
compound" 23–24
women, changing status
of 126–127
Wordsworth, William 27
writing, invention of in
Sumer 59

Y

Yeats, W.B. 74, 123
yidam 93
Yoga and Samsara 56–57

Z

Zimmer, Heinrich 70, 120,
121, 123
zodiac 61

ABOUT NEW DIMENSIONS

Inspired by the need for an overview of the dramatic cultural shifts and changing human values occurring on a planetary scale, New Dimensions Foundation was conceived and founded in March 1973 as a public, nonprofit educational organization. Shortly thereafter, New Dimensions Radio began producing programming for broadcast in northern California. Since then, more than 4,000 broadcast hours of programming intended to empower and enlighten have been produced. In 1980, "New Dimensions" went national via satellite as a weekly one-hour, in-depth interview series. More than 300 stations have aired the series since its inception, and "New Dimensions" has reached literally millions of listeners with its upbeat, practical, and provocative views of life and the human spirit.

Widely acclaimed as a unique and professional production, New Dimensions Radio programming has featured hundreds of the leading thinkers, social innovators, and visionaries of our time in far-ranging dialogues covering the major issues of this era. The interviews with Joseph Campbell from which this book was compiled are representative.

As interviewer and host, Michael Toms brings a broad background of knowledge and expertise to the "New Dimensions" microphones. His sensitive and engaging interviewing style as well as his own intellect and breadth of interests have been acclaimed by listeners and guests alike.

New Dimensions Radio provides a new model for exploring ideas in a spirit of open dialogue. Programs are produced to include the listener as an active participant as well as respecting the listener's intelligence and capacity for thoughtful choice. The programs are alive with dynamic spontaneity. "New Dimensions" programming celebrates life and the human spirit while challenging the mind to open to fresh possibilities. We invite your participation with us in the ultimate human adventure—the quest for wisdom and the inexpressible.

For a free *New Dimensions Newsletter*, a list of radio stations currently broadcasting the "New Dimensions" radio series, or a tape catalog, please write New Dimensions Radio, P.O. Box 410510, San Francisco, CA 94141, or you may telephone (415)563-8899.

THE "NEW DIMENSIONS" TAPES
WITH JOSEPH CAMPBELL

These tapes are the word-for-word recordings of the original conversations from which *An Open Life* was compiled.

Myths, Personal Dreams, and Universal Themes
The foremost teller of mythological tales shares his vast insight into the realm of myth, the unconscious, and the life of the spirit. From his childhood experience of "Buffalo Bill's Wild West Show" and his youthful wanderings through the Totem room of the American Museum of Natural History to his deep explorations of the Arthurian legend, Jung's psychology, Oriental philosophies, and the Judeo-Christian tradition, Campbell provides a wealth of wisdom. Highlight: his answer to the question "What happens after death?"
(Tape 1012, 2 hrs. $15)

Mythological Musings
A delightful and informal visit with a master storyteller who portrays the world through the two-way mirror of myth. Highlights include his views on the Apocalypse, God as personality, the Bible as metaphor, the collective unconscious, and Asian migration to the Americas. This conversation was recorded in a living room, so there is a "homey feel" to the

exchange between Campbell and three friends—interviewers Brunsman, Noffke, and Toms.　　　(Tape 1040, 2 hrs. $15)

Beyond Dogma: The Vision Quest Experience
Religion versus science, King Arthur's Court, Black Elk, UFOs, new discoveries about prehistory, artists as heroes, women's potential, the challenge of marriage, Oriental gurus, moon landings . . . these topics are brought to life in new ways by Campbell, who vividly and magically describes our planetary ancestral roots. This is a remarkable dialogue, with echoes from the past pointing to new possibilities in the present.　　　(Tape 1296, 2 hrs. $15)

The Myth of the Fool and Other Tales
This is a *tour de force* by Campbell, who leads us on a mythic journey from the emergence of Cro-Magnon man to Jung's "collective unconscious." Highlights: the early origins of cities and civilization; the nature of cults and gurus; the influence of Freud and Jung on his own work; the basic motifs of myth; the failure of modern religion; shamanic lore; finding one's own authentic path; the roles of the Hero and the Fool.
　　　(Tape 1374, 2 hrs. $15)

Ancient Voices
A journey into the farther reaches of our deeper selves: on this tape, Campbell shows both how myth is always with us and how understanding the past can unlock the doors to fully experiencing the present.　　　(Tape 1561, 1 hr. $9.95)

Conversation with Joseph Campbell
Have we lost our mythic heritage? Where are our heroes? Is our future contained in our past? Professor Campbell explores the inner link between our human lives and our human myths, revealing the myriad ways in which myth can enrich and magnify human existence.　　　(Tape 1586, 2 hrs. $15)

Joseph Campbell: Man of a Thousand Myths

"Myths are not invented like stories," says Joseph Campbell, "Myths are inspired. They come from the same realm that dreams come from." Close your eyes and enter the archetypal realm of the human psyche with a master guide.

(Tape 1709, 1 hr. $9.95)

Myth As Metaphor

Recorded when Joseph Campbell was eighty years old, just after he completed *The Way of the Animal Powers*. From understanding our relationships to probing the depths of our religious heritage and spiritual roots, this dialogue is a mythic journey across the barriers of time and space to long-forgotten eddies in the primal pool of our collective past. Professor Campbell shares a plethora of wisdom in this conversation.

(Tape 1848, 1 hr. $9.95)

Call of the Hero

Heeding the Call of the ultimate adventure, embracing one's own personal destiny, is the underlying theme of this wisdom-packed dialogue. "Follow your bliss," says Campbell, and a world of magic and fulfillment will open up to you. This is the call of the spirit, the journey of the hero with a thousand faces.

(Tape 1901, 1 hr. $9.95)

To Order Tapes

Mail check or money order (with Visa or MC give expiration date) and add $1 ($2 foreign and Canada) for first tape ordered for postage and handling. For each additional tape in the same shipment, add 50 cents for U.S. delivery, $1 for foreign and Canada. California residents add 6% sales tax (Bart counties 6½%). Send to New Dimensions Tapes, P.O. Box 410510, San Francisco, CA 94141. (Telephone: 415-563-8899)